MUSTANG
From *Wild* Horse to Riding Horse

One Trainer's Journal:
Groundwork, First Rides, Obstacles,
Trail Work, Liberty, Performance, and More

Vivian Gabor

Translated by Helen McKinnon

TRAFALGAR SQUARE
North Pomfret, Vermont

First published in the United States of America in 2020 by
Trafalgar Square Books
North Pomfret, Vermont 05053

Originally published in the German language as *Vom Wildpferd Zum Reitpferd* by Müller Rüschlikon Verlag, Stuttgart, an imprint of Paul Pietsch Verlag GmbH & Co. KG

Library of Congress Control Number: 2019956378

Photographs by Juliane Fellner, www.equus-foto.de, except Dr. Vivian Gabor (pp. 2, 3, 5, 7, 9, 10, 11, 12, 13, 15, 17, 19, 22, 23, 25, 26, 27, 29, 31, 34, 41, 43, 45, 48, 49, 52, 148, 149; Joanna Grüger (pp. 75, 76, 77, 78, 79); Nele Koblitz (pp. 87, 88, 89); Nicole Reitemeyer (pp. 137, 139, 141 bottom right, 142, 143, 144, 145 top left, 146, 147); Maggie Rothauge (pp. v, vi, 1, 152, 153); Victoria Shamraeva, www.equus-language.com (pp. 138, 140, 141, 144 small, 145).

Interior design by r2 | Ravenstein, Verden

Cover design by RM Didier

Index by Andrea Jones (JonesLiteraryServices.com)

Printed in the United States of America

10 9 8 7 6 5 4 3 2 1

CONTENTS

PREFACE

Neither starting a young horse over the course of three months nor preparing for a clinic or show is out of the ordinary for me as a trainer. The special thing about the challenge I write about in this book, however, was that the young horse I was training was an American Mustang, born in the wild and completely unused to humans, unlike our domestic horses.

I became involved in the "Mustang Makeover" in Germany, which is organized by "American Mustang Germany" (www.american-mustang.de), a group that is working to bring attention to the plight of the Mustang in the wild, as well as those in holding facilities. For the Makeover in Germany, between 15 and 20 Mustangs are imported from a holding facility and made available to trainers who have been vetted and selected to work with them. For 90 days, the trainers have the challenge of helping their wild horses become accustomed to the new environment, to people, and to the process of saddle training. At the end of this three-month training period, there is a large competition with almost 6,000 people in the audience to experience the event live and at the end, maybe bid for a Mustang in a special auction. The Makeover in Germany is also watched by approximately 40,000 fans on social media, so not only are a number of Mustangs given new homes, but many new people are introduced to the problems Mustangs face and how different organizations are trying to solve them. Those interested can follow along with all the participating trainers and experience the exciting progress made with each Mustang over the 90 days. So the Makeover is an event that shows a variety of training methods and encourages thought and discussion regarding the kinds of techniques you would like to use with your own horse.

When I first heard about the Mustang Makeover, I was interested to work with a wild horse, not only as a horse trainer, but also as a behavioral biologist and equine scientist. I like to teach others about horse-appropriate training methodology, but I also like to educate myself and face new, intriguing tasks and challenges. I consider myself fortunate to have been given a chance to be involved in this special adventure.

Was working with a Mustang really a completely different experience? This is something people have often asked me, both during and after the project. My spontaneous answer is and always will be, "Yes!"

The 90 days with "my" Mustang mare was a very intense time, during which I learned an incredible amount, because even when I wasn't actually training her, I was very closely involved with her and the issue of Mustangs as a whole. As well as learning about the background and origin of these horses, my time with one of them, above all, taught me about the true, unadulterated nature of horses. I realized that unlike our domesticated horses, Mustangs have not been bred with our interests and desires in mind. Nature's external influences are responsible for which in their wild herds survive.

The Makeover also taught me to look at some aspects of horse training and how we deal with horses from a completely different perspective—the horse's perspective. I had the opportunity to experience the pure nature of my wild horse, with all the good qualities and difficulties that came with it.

Would I do it again? "Yes!" is my unequivocal answer. The 90 days I spent working with a Mustang were special. They opened my eyes in many respects, and took me farther along my path toward species-appropriate treatment of horses and allowed me to further explore their nature. It wasn't an easy time, physically or emotionally. Nevertheless, I would do it all again in a heartbeat. I'm so glad that I had the opportunity to get to know "my" Mustang.

Dr. Vivian Gabor

INTRODUCTION

MUSTANGS IN AMERICA

Any romantic notions associated with the word "Mustang" are quickly shattered when you start to examine the problem of Mustangs in America. These feral horses are the descendants of horses taken there by Spanish explorers in the sixteenth century, and later, early American settlers.

At the start of the 1960s, large numbers of Mustangs were captured and slaughtered, pushing them to the brink of extinction. The subsequent ban on slaughter of Mustangs led to uncontrolled growth in their population, and the food available wasn't enough to support them. At the end of the 1980s, the BLM (Bureau of Land Management) established the first holding facilities where captured Mustangs were given the essentials. In North America, there are currently over 50,000 Mustangs living in the wild, and 45,000 in holding facilities. The "Appropriate Management Level" (AML) indicates whether the ratio between food resources and number of animals is correct. This relationship would be balanced at around 27,000 animals, so the AML is currently being far exceeded. As a result, the land is becoming increasingly barren and the resources enough to feed even fewer animals. The Mustang population doubles every four years, and severe overgrazing results in animals dying of starvation.

Around 10,000 horses are caught every year in the United States, but only 5,000 find homes. "Mustang Makeovers" are held to facilitate and speed up adoption of captured Mustangs. Trainers work with the Mustangs for a specific period before these events and then show off the Mustangs' skills to an audience to encourage them to buy the animals. These "adoptions" are a unique opportunity to give a "captured" Mustang a horse-friendly future worth living.

Horses and trainers are matched up at random—prospective owners pull toy horses with their Mustangs' TAG numbers (registration numbers) out of a box.

THE FIRST MONTH

1	2	3	4	5	6	7
8	9	10	11	12	13	14
15	16	17	18	19	20	21
22	23	24	25	26	27	28
29	30	31				

THE SECOND MONTH

		1	2	3	4	
5	6	7	8	9	10	11
12	13	14	15	16	17	18
19	20	21	22	23	24	25
26	27	28	29	30		

THE THIRD MONTH

					1	2
3	4	5	6	7	8	9
10	11	12	13	14	15	16
17	18	19	20	21	22	23
24	25	26	27	28	29	30
31						

THE MUSTANGS ARRIVE IN FRANKFURT

It feels strange to be driving to Frankfurt, Germany, knowing that I am going to be coming home with a Mustang. Actually being involved in this project still feels a little surreal to me. What will training a Mustang be like? Will it be similar or completely different from the horses I have dealt with so far? I don't think about it too much though, because I don't have a clue what direction the coming months will take.

I arrive at Frankfurt Airport's "Animal Lounge," Europe's largest transit hub for live animals, at around 2:00 p.m. Every year, around 15,000 pets land and take off from here, including approximately 1,600 horses.

Once I have signed in, I am allowed to drive onto the site. A few trainers are already there. I don't know many of them personally, and I am very excited to see what they think. We all have to wait quite a while, and a lively exchange ensues. The press is there and interview the organizers and some of the trainers until it is finally time for the Mustangs to be drawn. The horses had already been "pre-sorted" to a certain extent in order to avoid physically larger trainers ending up with the smallest Mustangs. The draw is done in three groups. This is when we feel the first emotions. Some people actually get the horses they want and are overwhelmed. I don't think about which of the horses might suit me, but just let one come to me. Perhaps not necessarily a bay or a chestnut, I think, because special coloring would be eye-catching. In the end, I draw a chestnut: TAG 3219—the Mustang mare looks nice. She has a harmonious conformation and is slightly more compact than the others. Everyone is given a short message from the American trainer who got the horses used to loading, with a few lines about the character and peculiarities of the horse in question. My card reads: "She's a very unflappable, sweet mare, though she can sometimes be very 'mare-ish.' She is willing to try things out, but this has also included nipping. She can sometimes be stubborn, but on the whole she is very friendly. She is curious and will approach you."

Then, we have to wait some more. The horses had arrived in the morning and customs are still checking the papers. A few hours later, it is time to begin. We are given the transportation documents. The first Mustang comes and is loaded. Some trainers take one Mustang with them; others, like me, are transporting their own, plus another animal for a friend or colleague. Everything happens very calmly. We try to seem relaxed, despite our excitement, but the tension is still palpable. The horses are loaded without any stress. A woman from

TAG 3219

HMA Beaty Butte, Oregon

Gather Nov. 2015

Geb.: 2013

Sorrel

MUSTANG MAKEOVER

TEAM VIVIAN

This is the first picture I see of "my" Mustang mare. She was caught from the "Beaty Butte" herd in Oregon in 2015, two years before the Mustang Makeover. She was born in 2013.

The Mustangs load calmly. Our first journey together can begin.

the organization in charge is responsible for loading the horses. She accompanied the Mustangs on the flight from Atlanta, Georgia. The horses know her voice and follow her quietly into the trailers. No overreactions, no violent stampedes! Instead, they seem astonishingly calm.

From the "Animal Lounge" straight into the trailer. This is the first time I see "my" Mustang mare in person. The barriers on the trailer ensure that the horse walks safely into it.

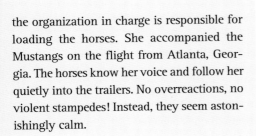

It's getting dark. It's a while before the majority of the 16 Mustangs are loaded and our two are on board. I feel excited as I catch sight of "my" Mustang for the first time, a brief first glance before the mare walks sweetly into the trailer. "She's familiar with food rewards," the organizer tells me. The trainer who prepared the Mustangs mentioned this to her specially. With a treat, the horse stands calmly in the trailer while the second horse is loaded. The back door of the trailer is then carefully closed, and I can travel home with "wild horses" on board.

As I am leaving Frankfurt, I am told that the American trainer had given my Mustang the name "Mona Lisa," which in my mind becomes simply "Mona."

There is some bumping and banging on the journey, but we don't have any problems. I feel more and more tension melt away. Exhausted after the long day, we finally arrive at the farm at half-past midnight. Zoe, the second trainer, is waiting, and we shepherd both mares from the trailer into their temporary stalls. That all goes smoothly, too. The mares immediately lower their heads and get down to the business of eating their hay. They are both very calm, as if nothing has happened.

GETTING TO KNOW YOU
The First Touch

I offer my Mustang mare the back of my hand and invite her to sniff it. Very hesitantly, Mona reaches her head in my direction. She is very cautious but also seems curious. The first, tentative touch happens!

I find the clip on Mona's halter and remove the lead rope. Doing this with the other Mustang is no problem either. It's bound to be a strange moment for both horses, because they have had the ropes on their halters continuously in recent weeks. However, Zoe and I wonder immediately afterward if we made the right decision! I'm very glad that there are two of us doing the Makeover and that we can talk about our feelings. We discuss how things might go with our Mustangs over the coming months.

It's very late, but we still spend some more time outside the stalls. Since the two mares will soon be separated (Zoe's Mustang is moving in two days), we put them in separate outdoor stalls. I am still interested in connecting and go into Mona's stall again; however, she doesn't give me a friendly greeting. In fact, she doesn't want me anywhere near her, and threatens me. I hadn't expected that: skepticism, yes, but more evasive, even anxious behavior. Zoe's mare reacts differently from Mona. She is very timid, and immediately avoids her when Zoe enters the stall.

The horses' different natures are already clear to see. Perhaps they had different previous experiences in the herd. Maybe Mona's defensive behavior has so far served her well. Who knows? Or is this typical Mustang behavior?

This first encounter and the mare's defensive behavior have given me food for thought. Will I be able to convince this horse to work with me? I start having doubts. Make Mona "rideable" within three months? I don't quite believe it yet. With these feelings, the first day with "my" Mustang comes to an end.

THE FIRST MONTH

1	2	3	4	5	6	7
8	9	10	11	12	13	14
15	16	17	18	19	20	21
22	23	24	25	26	27	28
29	30	31				

THE SECOND MONTH

			1	2	3	4
5	6	7	8	9	10	11
12	13	14	15	16	17	18
19	20	21	22	23	24	25
26	27	28	29	30		

THE THIRD MONTH

					1	2
3	4	5	6	7	8	9
10	11	12	13	14	15	16
17	18	19	20	21	22	23
24	25	26	27	28	29	30
31						

4

THE FIRST MONTH

WEEK 1

The two Mustang mares are still together. Zoe and I consider whether we will be able to separate them and lead them individually into the round pen. I am so excited about this first step in the horses' "work." We had taken the lead ropes off the halters the evening before, so to lead the horses, we need to put the ropes back on. The mares set us straight: Just clip a rope onto a Mustang's halter? No chance! There was a good reason why the American trainer, who had halter-broken them and prepared them for transport, left the ropes on the halters. Mona warily watches my cautious approach.

Because she doesn't immediately turn away, but stays standing curiously, I am actually able to clip the lead rope onto the ring of her halter after a few minutes. It takes a little longer with Zoe's cautious mare, but we have time.

It becomes clear to me during this first step of training that we can't achieve anything with speed. This project will remind me time and again to approach this horse calmly, circumspectly, and without time pressure. What an undertaking!

I take Mona out of her stall, while Zoe stays with the other Mustang mare. She isn't particularly bothered by the separation. I had expected a different reaction here, too.

The mares are relaxed and eating
in their temporary stall.

Despite having grown up naturally in a herd, both horses seem to have a certain degree of independence. I wonder whether even just this first calm approach has been enough to build up a relationship to a human. I would be surprised if it had because that would be incredibly fast.

Mona follows me quietly for the 50 yards or so to the round pen, looks around, but definitely doesn't go into flight mode. Everything is new to her: the buildings we walk between, the other horses in the exercise pen that she can see next to the round pen. Another 50 yards away is the large indoor arena—but this building doesn't seem to impress her either.

I enter the round pen ahead of her and she follows me willingly. How do you begin training a wild Mustang? I try to see Mona as a completely normal horse and think about what I would normally do.

I start with some simple exercises that are supposed to teach her to focus on me. I walk in circles and keep stopping and observing whether she is paying attention to me. I can see that she finds this difficult and keeps looking around her. As a result, she follows unsteadily, a little behind me. You couldn't call it normal leading. I notice that being led on a rope like this doesn't mean anything to her. Of course, she just isn't ready for it at the moment. And why should she be? I feel the urge to let her go. I consider for a moment whether that is wise, and what could happen. Our round pen is fenced with panels so, in principle, escape is impossible. It is possible that I won't be able to catch Mona again. However, as has been the case with other timid or anxious horses, good round-pen training makes it possible to build up a relationship with any horse that allows himself to be caught again. (Well, that's my theory, anyway.)

So I risk it and remove Mona's rope. Then, something astonishing happens. I had expected her to want to get away from me. I am familiar with that behavior from horses I have trained, when I "let them go" in the round pen. They run around and try to get the lay of the land. But not this Mustang mare—she just stays next to me when I unclip the rope. It simply does not occur to her to leave me or to run wildly around the round pen. I can't send her away from me. Instead, she is intent on staying by my side!

Nevertheless, I want to give her the opportunity to move away from me. That's what I would normally do when training a young horse. One of the reasons I do this is to establish my status as the "leader." The idea is that I determine speed and direction, and establish my position in the middle of the circle—in a space that the horse shouldn't enter without being asked. If I see that the horse is

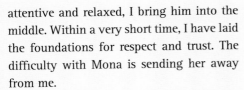

Mona follows me at liberty in the round pen for the first time. She seeks connection and contact.

attentive and relaxed, I bring him into the middle. Within a very short time, I have laid the foundations for respect and trust. The difficulty with Mona is sending her away from me.

I wonder how this can be possible as horses are supposed to be flight animals! I actually manage to send her into trot for at least a couple of yards then bring her back to me. She is soon following me freely for the first time after bringing her in the pen. What a moment!

Follow My Leader

"If you've got a clue then I'll follow you!" Horses have evolved to live together in a herd to ensure their survival. They are more likely to survive in a herd than alone. Coexistence in the herd is governed by hierarchies. This reduces risk of injury in the herd and clarifies allocation of responsibilities. An animal's status gives him additional security. Responsibility is given to higher-ranking animals, and young horses grow up under their protection. A high rank is obtained through physical fitness and experience. If we can manage to assume this protective role when training horses, the horse will happily follow us, and to a certain extent, hand over to us responsibility for his survival.

THE SECOND DAY

After yesterday's beautiful moment when Mona followed me, I go back into the round pen today. I start with work on the rope. The mare is very attentive, and I begin with basic exercises such as halting and backing up. When I stop, the horse must stop, too. If I stand in front of the horse and then walk toward her, she must move backward away from me. I feel that the basic attitude of giving me space is particularly important here, because Mona's curiosity always makes her want to approach me, which is lovely. I notice that she always responds to being sent out of my space with a change in facial expression. She is more likely to respond to physical pressure that is built up near her with resistance than with flight.

Fight or Flight: Why Flight Isn't Always the Best Option for Flight Animals

"Fight or flight" is the behavioral phenomenon that requires horses to quickly choose between fleeing or fighting. You would think that flight would always be the first option for a flight animal. However, every flight entails expending a lot of energy. If the threat can be quickly removed by fighting or defensive behavior, then this is the less costly option in terms of energy. Since energy is essential for surviving in the wild and must be built up laboriously by eating, defensive behavior can be a more economical and, therefore, safer decision.

THE FIRST MONTH

1	2	3	4	5	6	7
8	9	10	11	12	13	14
15	16	17	18	19	20	21
22	23	24	25	26	27	28
29	30	31				

THE SECOND MONTH

		1	2	3	4
5	6	7	8	9	10	11
12	13	14	15	16	17	18
19	20	21	22	23	24	25
26	27	28	29	30		

THE THIRD MONTH

					1	2
3	4	5	6	7	8	9
10	11	12	13	14	15	16
17	18	19	20	21	22	23
24	25	26	27	28	29	30
31						

In order to practice the principles of yielding with Mona, which is important for all further steps in her training, I try to get her to yield as follows: I direct my gaze at her hindquarters and turn in the direction of them. The sensitivity of Mona's reaction to my body language is astonishing. I hardly need to build up any muscular tension for her to understand what I want from her. I then walk in front of her in a small semi-circle and direct my gaze at her shoulder. Horses find exercises where they have to yield their forehand difficult because there is more weight on it. Moving the shoulders—shoulder control—is also more difficult during subsequent ridden work than controlling the hindquarters. Here, too, Mona is astonishingly quick to learn that every time she gives the correct response, I immediately leave her in peace by releasing my physical "pressure." These first steps happen within a few

I use my gaze and body language to get Mona to move her hindquarters away from me. If I focus on her hindquarters, the mare naturally understands which part of her body to move. This worked without lengthy preparatory training.

Learning in the Wild

Learning is defined as adapting to changing environmental conditions. The ability to learn throughout a lifetime is, therefore, an essential mechanism for survival, and crucial for a wild horse who roams through different habitats.

The ability to adapt quickly and respond appropriately to new environmental stimuli has become highly developed over generations of Mustangs. The ability to tell whether a stimulus is relevant or irrelevant—that is, threatening or non-threatening—is an important mechanism for conserving vital energy and not squandering it on often unnecessary flight.

minutes. I realize that I am dealing with a horse that picks up new things incredibly quickly. When a horse has understood the point of the exercise, that is, that the right response relieves the pressure, he will be motivated and attentive.

I introduce praise: when the mare gives the correct response and I finish the signal, I say, "Good," in a high-pitched voice. This gives me a way of quickly confirming that her reaction was correct for new exercises and also from the saddle (see the principle

The first lateral steps happen spontaneously. I give the horse the signal to yield by looking at her belly and slightly raising my driving whip hand.

of "Secondary Reinforcer" below). During this 20-minute session and after just two repetitions, Mona actually manages to take two steps over with her forehand and her hindquarters. She always seems motivated to pay attention to me when she is working. I risk an attempt, look at her belly and walk a few steps along an imaginary line in front of her. She actually understands me and begins to cross over sideways two steps with her forehand and hindquarters.

Praise:
The Secondary Reinforcer

A secondary reinforcer is like a bridge between the right reaction and the reward. The reinforcer, usually a sound (click or word of praise) shows that a reaction was desired at a certain moment. However, the secondary reinforcer must previously have been associated with a reward, such as food or a break. This enables you to directly reward a behavior but slightly delay giving the actual reward. When training young horses, it makes sense to work with a word that can be used later on for other new exercises, even if the secondary reinforcer isn't always followed by a food reward.

The speed at which this untouched horse picks it up tells me that the signals that I have learned from training many "normal" young horses also work for her and are communicable. It's a wonderful feeling. These signals also seem to be understood more quickly by a wild horse than by our domesticated horses.

On day two, the second Mustang mare travels to her temporary home. We load her slowly, which works well. I stand by Mona's stall for a few minutes after the other mare leaves. She does not appear agitated or upset. I don't have any problem leading her out in her halter and taking her to her new paddock and stall, where she will live for the next three months. Once again, this horse surprises me. Mona walks

Mona's first contact with a "non-Mustang" is relaxed.

into the new stall, looks around, has a brief sniff at her neighbor—a Friesian—then focuses on her pile of hay. I am astounded by the way she deals with new surroundings but, when I think about it, it makes sense not to waste valuable energy getting worked up over every new but not obviously dangerous thing. Who knows when and for what you might need this energy?

THE THIRD DAY

I spend far more time around Mona than I normally would with horses I am training. Sometimes I just stand in front of her paddock stall and watch her eat. And she is always eating. It seems as if she would just swallow up anything she can get. It's no surprise when you consider that every type of food is valuable in the wild. A wild horse doesn't know how long food will last and when he will next have to use up the valuable energy the food provides for flight or fight.

I think about what else I can feed her. On the one hand, the food has to make sense in terms of energy, but on the other, it mustn't be too much for her body as we have been told she is only used to grass, hay, and alfalfa. I decide to give her dried alfalfa to keep "feeding her up." She wasn't too thin when she arrived from America, but a little more bulk and energy—including for building muscle—can't do any harm. There is already a salt lick in her stall.

Today, I continue our training in the round pen. I let her walk around me at liberty to begin with, but it is quite difficult to get her to go "forward." She goes back to walk as soon as I lower my body tension when sending her forward. Inviting her back in to me works quite well, because it gives her a break.

I lower my body tension as soon as the Mustang mare relaxes and lowers her head in walk or trot. She makes the connection between lowering her head and praise, and learns to adopt a relaxed, low head carriage more and more.

She readily accepts breaks as a reward. She pays incredibly close attention to my body language, so I now show her that I immediately tone down my body tension as soon as she slightly lowers her head in trot.

Again, all it takes is a few repetitions where the tendency to lower her head and my relaxed posture as a reward come together for her to understand what I want from her.

ALLOWING TOUCH

I try to touch Mona's body more and more frequently. She doesn't really like being touched. Why would she? She isn't familiar with it. My touches don't make any sense to her. Apart from another horse,

Conditioning: Rewarding a Chance Behavior

Conditioning is when a behavior that is initially shown at random is reinforced—that is, deliberately shown more frequently—by repeated association with a positive outcome (operant conditioning). A direct signal—for example, touching the horse's poll to get him to lower his head (see p. 14)—can gradually be changed but continues to retain its meaning (classical conditioning).

what other animal would touch a horse in the wild? Contact with another species would only happen in an attack. If horses touch each other during mutual grooming, for example, this is always preceded by certain gestures. A horse will approach slowly and enquiringly, and mutual grooming only begins if the other horse consents. We take it for granted that we can just walk up to our horses and touch them. We should definitely think about this and realize what it means for them.

Mona shows me clearly that she doesn't enjoy my touch, even if I approach her very cautiously. I assume that she can't work out what the point is. Her expression changes and she quickly sends threatening signals in my direction. I don't allow myself to be intimidated, but consciously relax and touch her shoulder-wither area with slow, stroking movements. I stop touching her as soon as

Mona is apprehensive about direct contact, as clearly shown by the position of her ears and head. I take up a relaxed posture and slowly feel my way forward. She finds it easier to tolerate her legs being touched with the end of the whip than direct contact with my hand.

her expression relaxes. The idea is to show Mona that she has a say in the decision and that I won't force her to do anything. She should realize that acceptance and relaxation, not defense, are the solutions for influencing me.

I only get her to "tolerate" this exercise for seconds, before returning to yielding exercises.

YIELDING TO PRESSURE

I think it is extremely important to teach horses that are around people the basic principle of yielding to pressure as early as possible. I don't just mean the subsequent pressure on the reins or pressure from the rider's leg, but also the physical pressure and physical tension that the handler builds up from the ground. In the wild, higher-ranking horses would tell lower-ranking horses to move away by changing their expression, gestures, and physical tension. It is really easy for horses to transfer this to people, because it is how they naturally communicate.

Yesterday, I laid the foundations for this with Mona by getting her to yield her hindquarters and forehand. Today, I repeat these exercises with and without the rope. I don't need the rope, because Mona wants to be close to me, follows me at liberty and, to my amazement, immediately starts doing the exercises from yesterday. She tries especially hard to step right over with her front legs if I immediately say the praise word "Good!" and remove the physical pressure. Stepping over to the side with her forehand and hindquarters works right away, too. My gaze and the alignment of my body tell the mare where my focus is. It feels great that this communication method is instantly understood by this untrained horse. What I'm doing is logical to Mona!

I try another exercise with her that is firstly supposed to be about yielding to gentle pressure and, secondly, to mean that I can always get her to relax: head-lowering.

I give gentle downward pulses on the rope with one hand, and touch Mona's poll with the other. The reaction that follows is stronger than I have ever seen in a domesticated horse. As soon as I build up gentle pressure on her poll musculature with my fingers, she violently shakes her head as if an annoying insect had bitten the crest of her mane. Because of her reaction, I could have quickly taught her to perform the trick "Say no," but I obviously don't!

I don't let her "shake off" my hand, but maintain the light contact with her poll. Now all she has to do is show the "right" reaction—in this case, move her head away from the pressure toward the ground. And

THE FIRST MONTH

1 2 3 4 5 6
8 9 10 11 12 13 14
15 16 17 18 19 20 21
22 23 24 25 26 27 28
29 30 31

THE SECOND MONTH

1 2 3 4
5 6 7 8 9 10 11
12 13 14 15 16 17 18
19 20 21 22 23 24 25
26 27 28 29 30

THE THIRD MONTH

1 2
3 4 5 6 7 8 9
10 11 12 13 14 15 16
17 18 19 20 21 22 23
24 25 26 27 28 29 30
31

Being touched on her poll initially triggers Mona's uncertainty and counter-pressure (photo 1). She then uses defensive behavior—nipping my arm—to get rid of the pressure (photo 2). I stay relaxed, maintain the gentle pressure on her and wait for the right reaction (photo 3). A few seconds later, she lowers her head, and I immediately remove the pressure exerted by my fingers (photo 4).

would you believe it, a few seconds later, she hits upon the idea of doing just that. I stop touching her immediately.

Later, in the saddle, the "head-lowering" exercise will be extremely important to me, because it allows me to get the horse to assume a relaxed posture at any time.

Head–Lowering for Relaxation

If the body is put into a relaxed position, the brain follows by excreting relaxing chemicals. Posture and mind then interact. Lowered head posture, which goes hand in hand with relaxation of the back and neck muscles, usually occurs when the horse is dozing or eating—that is, when there is no threat of danger. The brain, therefore, puts the horse in a comfortable physical state. You can not only use this posture in training, but also condition it, which means that you make relaxation reproducible.

THE FOURTH DAY

Mona is still wearing her green halter from America. I haven't tried to take it off. She does let me touch her head, but it is still too tricky for me to take it off completely. I have swapped the long lead rope that was on her halter with a shorter piece of rope. The advantage of this is that I don't have to actually touch her head with my hand to clip on a different rope. Mona watches my approaching hands warily, so the short rope is the best solution for us for the time being.

Today, I take a video of Mona in the round pen. The video is about habituation and sensitization. In it, I record the most essential principles that are important to me when I start training a horse. The horse should pay attention to my signals, especially the tension in my body, because she will naturally recognize them. I want Mona to react sensitively to my signal to yield. The precise increase in my body tension should encourage her to yield. On the other hand, Mona should not overreact in response to unfamiliar situations or supposedly scary objects, but preferably become even more relaxed if I convey this to her with my minimal muscular tension.

Horses Naturally Pay Attention to Body Tension

In a wild herd, paying attention to the signals and, therefore, the body language of the other horses, is vitally important. The entire herd will be ready to run within a few seconds of a threat being perceived. The muscles tense and stimulants such as adrenaline are excreted to prepare the horse optimally for flight. This herd synchronization is vital to horses' survival. Taking on the calm and relaxation of the other herd members when no danger is imminent is equally important. That is the time when horses can relax and gather their energy for the next time danger threatens.

HABITUATION EXERCISES

To get Mona more used to touch, I stroke the mare with the handle end of the whip. It's a little bigger than the other end and is supposed to give her trust in my touch. I use the whip as an extension of my own body.

THE FIRST MONTH

1	2	3	4	5	6	7
8	9	10	11	12	13	14
15	16	17	18	19	20	21
22	23	24	25	26	27	28
29	30	31				

THE SECOND MONTH

			1	2	3	4
5	6	7	8	9	10	11
12	13	14	15	16	17	18
19	20	21	22	23	24	25
26	27	28	29	30		

THE THIRD MONTH

					1	2
3	4	5	6	7	8	9
10	11	12	13	14	15	16
17	18	19	20	21	22	23
24	25	26	27	28	29	30
31						

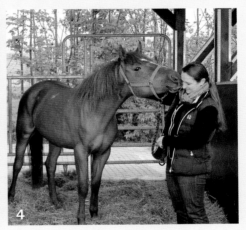

Being approached in her stall initially triggers apprehension and defensive behavior. For this reason, it is easier to carefully bring her to me using the short rope.

The rope isn't necessary at liberty in the round pen where Mona is more relaxed about being approached and touched. She feels less hemmed in here than in the stall.

This helps me to be able to relax my own posture so that I can touch the horse all over. I notice that touching her with the whip or with the longer, soft groundwork (lunge) rope triggers less tension and apprehension in Mona than touching her with my hand. This seems logical, as you can communicate tension through equipment, but body tension is communicated much more directly with your own body.

Why Touching a Horse Isn't Normal

Being touched by an animal other than a horse basically means danger for a horse in the wild. As I already mentioned, being touched by a predator, snake, or insect has negative connotations. So, if you want to touch a young horse, or a horse that is not familiar with human contact, you should always remember that this type of approach and contact is not natural for him!

In my training today, I stroke Mona with the whip for a few moments. She shouldn't show a reaction as I do so. I then change my body language slightly and get the horse to yield her hindquarters or forehand. This change is supposed to teach Mona to get better and better at assessing my actions. She should be able to rely on her ability to read and understand me correctly. This will enable me to make my stimuli more and more subtle.

After the habituation exercises that she has done very well today, I expand my training with a "scary object" in the form of a plastic bag.

I don't approach Mona head-on with this new object, because she would immediately perceive it as a threat. Instead, I take her by the lead rope and walk in front of her with the screwed up plastic bag. I notice that she doesn't know what to make of this unfamiliar object and probably won't easily allow it near her. By walking along in front of her, I show Mona that the object essentially moves away from her when she approaches it. The worst thing that could happen to a flight animal is for him to run and the object to follow. For that reason, I would never tie or attach a frightening object to a horse.

THE FIRST MONTH

1 2 3 4 5 6 7
8 9 10 11 12 13 14
15 16 17 18 19 20 21
22 23 24 25 26 27 28
29 30 31

THE SECOND MONTH

            1   2   3   4
5   6   7   8   9 10 11
12 13 14 15 16 17 18
19 20 21 22 23 24 25
26 27 28 29 30

THE THIRD MONTH

                    1   2
3   4   5   6   7   8   9
10 11 12 13 14 15 16
17 18 19 20 21 22 23
24 25 26 27 28 29 30
31

18

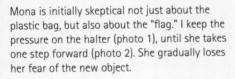

Mona is initially skeptical not just about the plastic bag, but also about the "flag." I keep the pressure on the halter (photo 1), until she takes one step forward (photo 2). She gradually loses her fear of the new object.

I then try approaching Mona's shoulder at an angle with the plastic bag. As I approach her, I have my head lowered and I turn away from her slightly to convey low tension. The plastic bag is still screwed up into a ball. I hold it in my hand. I am using the principle of "overshadowing" here. A stimulus, in this case being stroked by my hand, is overshadowed by a "new" stimulus—the contact with the plastic bag that I am gradually adding. When Mona notices this, she takes a massive leap to the side!

Soon we are in a position where I am looking at her with the plastic bag, and she is trying to get away from me by going backward. I use pressure on the halter to prevent her from getting any farther away, quietly resist and try to relax my posture again.

Mona's violent reaction has given me a fright. I let her relieve the pressure in my direction by taking a small step toward me, and immediately praise her. Now she is obviously "forewarned"—I would not have expected such a strong reaction. I try the approach for the second time, and again, contact with the object triggers a short "panic" attack. What's astounding is that, on the whole, Mona is neither upset nor frantic. The defensive/flight reaction is in response to the frightening object alone. I have known other young horses stay frantic or become even more wound up when they overreact to an unfamiliar object. That is not the case here.

Mona moves backward again to escape the situation after being touched. At this moment I change tactic slightly. If this "passive" touch isn't working for her, I try a cooperative principle. When there is still tension on the rope, I don't keep the bag still. On the contrary, I start to move it. I have been bringing Mona to me by looking at her shoulder, and I now use this technique in parallel.

Mona initially tries to put even more distance between herself and the moving object. I resist for a few seconds, and bring her to me with my gaze at her shoulder and the circular movement that I would normally make with a whip. It works. She decreases the pressure on the halter for a fraction of a second, and at that point, I am immediately still. I give her several inches of rope, immediately lower the plastic bag, and praise the horse effusively with my voice. Then, I gently circle the bag again while looking at Mona's shoulder, and use my body language to signal a backward movement. It takes two to three seconds, but then Mona takes a step toward me. I now move backward more actively to show her that her movement toward the frightening object makes it move away. It also stops circling and doesn't make any noise. She picks it up very quickly.

After a few repetitions, we are in a better place with the plastic bag. She still isn't relaxed about accepting the contact today, but I have laid important foundations for it. I won't force Mona to do anything, but I praise her willingness to cooperate and find solutions to problems. She shouldn't just panic and flee but instead actively deal with the object. This is extremely important for subsequent situations with people, both on the ground and under saddle, because horses will always encounter things they find strange.

On the way back from the round pen to the stall, I let Mona pluck at the grass for the first time. I want to get her used to grass gradually, because her digestive system isn't accustomed to our lush green stuff yet.

THE FIRST MONTH

1	2	3	4	5	6	
8	9	10	11	12	13	14
15	16	17	18	19	20	21
22	23	24	25	26	27	28
29	30	31				

THE SECOND MONTH

			1	2	3	4
5	6	7	8	9	10	11
12	13	14	15	16	17	18
19	20	21	22	23	24	25
26	27	28	29	30		

THE THIRD MONTH

					1	2
3	4	5	6	7	8	9
10	11	12	13	14	15	16
17	18	19	20	21	22	23
24	25	26	27	28	29	30
31						

Introducing her to grazing is also a very important phase for her. She is skeptical to begin with and tries the grass cautiously. However, once she tries it, her doubts vanish. This caution is not something normally seen in our domesticated horses. Even though eating is essential for the Mustang mare's survival, she is circumspect to begin with, because it might be dangerous for her. After the first taste she seems to have developed a liking for grass because everything green that she meets on her way magically attracts her. This again shows the importance of food as a resource for wild horses. They want to fill up their energy stores wherever possible.

SKEPTICISM ABOUT STRANGE FOOD

To get Mona used to me and my touch, and so that she associates me with something positive, I offer her a horse treat. Interestingly, caution wins over greed, because she doesn't accept it! I try an apple—something natural. Mona takes the unknown food cautiously but immediately spits it out. This is probably because of the juicy consistency that she initially finds strange, but it could also be the sweet taste. Horses can differentiate between many different tastes, but familiarity and habituation also seem to play a major role. For horses, familiar means "safe." Again, this caution shows me how closely connected she is with nature. We aren't sure whether our domesticated horses can identify poisonous plants as such. Have they lost this natural protection? We try to keep them away from any poisonous grasses and bushes, because we often don't believe that they possess this natural caution. I think that the difference between horses that grow up in the wild and our horses

is that, in the wild, it is always possible to move on and not have to eat whatever is still growing in a confined paddock or bare pasture. On the other hand, this important resource—their food—is served up to them several times a day, so the ability to decide and to look out for themselves is maybe even "trained out" of them. This results in horses that just want to eat anything that looks green or anything in the feed room. You should be aware that, by keeping horses in a restricted space, we are depriving them of a natural and very sensitive decision-making ability.

THE FIFTH DAY
An Important Foundation— Allowing Handling

When you are going to "use" a horse for pleasure riding, one of the most important things that he has to learn is to be touched by people and to be confronted with things that he would never encounter in the wild. You have a responsibility to get the horse used to objects and situations so that he is not constantly under stress thinking he has to flee or continually defend himself. This is not only important for handling, groundwork, or riding, but also so that you can look after his health and his feet.

Healthcare wasn't great in the corrals where the Mustangs had spent the past two years. Their hooves could no longer wear down as they would have in the wild, and I could see that in Mona's feet, too.

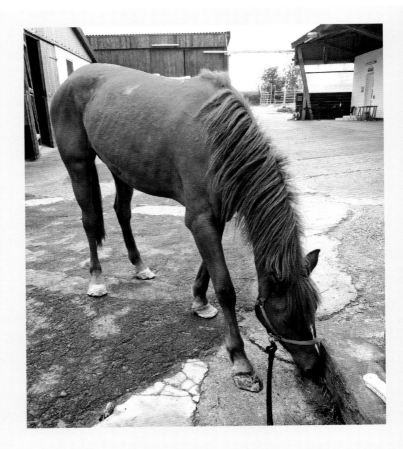

Mona's hooves have not been able to wear down naturally during the past two years in captivity. The farrier needs to work on the mare's feet soon, as a matter of urgency.

I consider one of my most important jobs to be preparing Mona for her life with us. As I've said, this includes allowing herself to be handled and touched—preferably all over—before even thinking about riding. Obviously it makes no sense for a wild horse to tolerate being touched by a human, which might, in the case of wound care, even be painful for him. That makes specific preparation all the more important.

Mona has a small wound on her lower jaw, because the halter that she has been wearing for a long time rubs against it when she chews. This open wound is constantly being irritated. I was able to loosen her halter slightly on the first day. Today I am able to carefully dab some wound cream onto the affected area, which will certainly have briefly been painful for her, but she tolerates it. I hope that I will soon be able to remove the halter completely.

That's why I keep working on handling, and today we go back into the round pen, where I can work with new objects in a small area. The round pen gives horses a sense of security, because its boundary constitutes a safe area for them, but they can still be aware of everything that goes on around them. They learn to focus on the stimuli coming from me, despite any external stimuli. I immediately praise them for this. This is what I do with Mona. After a few days, she is familiar with work in the round pen, and I can gradually do new habituation exercises with her.

I touch her shoulders and back with the lead rope, and stroke it over her croup. I then put the lead rope over Mona's back and allow her to walk around after me. The rope swings gently against her barrel. The object stays on her, but I want her to realize that it isn't dangerous. I walk calmly in front of her and praise her as we go. My gaze directed at her shoulder and the whip, which is pointing in this direction, are enough to signal to her that she should keep coming toward me. This gives her something to do, and the loose rope on her back fades into the background.

Paying Attention to the Handler in Unfamiliar Situations

The method of getting a horse to concentrate on me when he encounters something new or frightening has proven itself. A horse can only pay attention to one thing so I direct his attention to me and my signals. It also habituates the horse to the new object or situation. The horse learns more and more to focus on the person and to trust her, even in situations where he feels unsure.

When habituating her to the rope, I do what I did with the plastic bag and encourage Mona to actively cooperate. She has already accepted touch on her back and belly. However, it is important to me that she experience more and more situations that might initially trigger apprehension but then—a short time later—end well. This lets me teach her that, if she encounters something unexpected, the solution is to pay attention to the human's behavior. The more often this principle is effective, the more reliably the horse will follow it. How do I deal with the scary object? Am I tense or relaxed? If the horse learns to understand my intention, she will be able to follow me in these moments, too.

The right mix of apprehension and curiosity helps horses to survive in the wild. Both of these behaviors are very pronounced in Mona. I give her enough time to get to know her new environment.

I move the lead rope in front of Mona, starting small and then gradually increasing the movements. The rope occasionally falls onto the ground and makes noises. I observe her closely. I want her to react and find a solution, but I only increase the stimuli cautiously. As with the plastic bag, the mare initially wants to escape this stimulus. She goes backward to put some distance between her and the rope. I use the same principle as the day before and swing the rope in the direction of her shoulder. My posture remains totally relaxed as I do so. Mona recognizes the same pattern and approaches the swinging object. I have to make sure that my posture is relaxed but also inviting. I adopt a slightly stooped posture and move backward, away from her. This creates room for her to approach me, and helps her to find a solution more quickly.

FIRST HOOF-HANDLING EXERCISES

When it comes to habituating Mona to having her feet picked up, I proceed with great caution. Mona has already become familiar with being stroked by the rope and the whip. It makes sense to use a whip for touching the legs for the first time, because it allows me to be slightly out of the "danger zone," especially at the hindquarters. I can also remain upright and don't need to assume a crouched position next to the horse that she might find threatening. At the moment, Mona is more comfortable if I don't touch her with my hands. I can also build up steady pressure over an area by stroking her with the whip. Horses tend to flinch from very light and delicate touch—we know this from how they twitch their skin or stamp their feet when a fly lands on their body. Because I obviously want to be able to touch Mona with my hand at some point, I use the "overshadowing" method. To overshadow a new stimulus, you use the appearance of a new—possibly frightening—stimulus, by drawing the horse's attention to a stimulus that they already know and do not respond to with flight or defense. In this case, I increasingly replace the repeated, impulse-like strokes with the whip (like brush strokes) with strokes with my hand. I gradually work my way down from the horse's elbow area to the sensitive areas on the cannon bone (see photos on p. 13).

If Mona finds something strange, I immediately notice the change in her expression and the tension in her face. The behavior is often accompanied by her laying her ears back and snapping with her teeth. I realize that she doesn't really want to bite me. She just reacts this way to tell me that this contact is new and unfamiliar to her and outside of her comfort zone, which she doesn't like. It's important that I don't

THE FIRST MONTH

1	2	3	4	5	6	7
8	9	10	11	12	13	14
15	16	17	18	19	20	21
22	23	24	25	26	27	28
29	30	31				

THE SECOND MONTH

			1	2	3	4
5	6	7	8	9	10	11
12	13	14	15	16	17	18
19	20	21	22	23	24	25
26	27	28	29	30		

THE THIRD MONTH

					1	2
3	4	5	6	7	8	9
10	11	12	13	14	15	16
17	18	19	20	21	22	23
24	25	26	27	28	29	30
31						

24

Mona greets the farrier curiously. Getting to know each other over the fence is the only item on the agenda today.

reinforce her behavior and remove the contact if possible. I leave her in peace as soon as she tolerates my touch on her leg for one or two seconds. She understands this approach very quickly. Today, I even manage to get her to briefly lift her front hooves, and then praise her immediately.

I am aware how much trust Mona is already showing me. Losing her contact with the ground, and the stability that goes with it, constitutes a very big loss of control for a wild horse. When a horse is standing on four legs, she can immediately use her most important means of flight and defense. When you consider that I'm putting my hand around the leg, which is what a predator might do with its mouth, then the gravity of what I'm asking for from the horse becomes clear.

THE FARRIER MEETS THE MUSTANG

I am fortunate enough to work with a farrier who makes time for a project like this,

without doing his actual job: working on the horse's feet. Today, the Mustang and the farrier meet for the first time over the paddock fence. Mona approaches him curiously and sniffs his hand. I realize how important it is that this horse hasn't built up any negative associations with people, unlike the horses I normally work with. Constant curiosity seems to be deeply rooted in this wild horse and often supersedes her apprehension.

Curiosity Ensures Survival

Curiosity is a horse's essential drive to explore his world. He sizes up what could possibly be dangerous, but also what could help his survival. It could be a new source of food or water, but also an encounter with a horse that might become a new companion. Curiosity is closely linked with learning behavior and dealing with new situations. Being curious enough to assess an unfamiliar situation is, therefore, important for survival.

The green halter is finally off! Mona investigates the new bridle with curiosity. She even puts her nose through it as if she knows what it is for.

THE SIXTH DAY

Taking off the Halter for the First Time

After Mona has worn her halter for almost an entire week, today we managed it. She has been getting better and better at being touched on her head and allowing me to care for the wound on her lower jaw. I've found her a new bridle that can be used as a halter, as well as for work as a cavesson, and later, for riding. It is made of soft Bio-Thane® webbing with extra padding in sensitive areas, such as the jaw, nose, and poll. Its major advantage is that the headpiece fastens over the poll with a buckle at the side, so you don't have to pull it over the horse's ears every time you put it on and take it off. Mona still finds movements near her head threatening.

I start by hanging the bridle in her paddock. I don't know how she will react to the new object, so I don't want to overwhelm her. Her curiosity wins again. Mona investigates the new object and actually sticks her nose into the noseband. Allowing her to explore this new thing without forcing her gives the mare confidence.

I hold the bridle and stroke Mona's neck with it. She can then approach it by herself. As soon as her nose is even slightly in the noseband, I slowly take the bridle away from her again. I don't want to overwhelm her, but show her that interacting with the object is the right decision. She has to understand that she always has a way out and that cooperating won't result in her being trapped, so she becomes more and more curious. Putting her nose into the bridle is still her decision for the time being.

Outsmarting Destroys Trust

Far too often, people are too quick to exploit a moment—whether during loading, saddling for the first time, or even putting on a foal's first halter. This causes the horse to quickly lose trust in the human's actions. In this case, being outsmarted only shows the horse that cooperating, being curious, or even listening to the person is punished. The feeling of self-efficacy is taken away from the horse.

The Feeling of Self-Efficacy

Even if we can't say precisely how horses feel, we can definitely ascribe to them the ability to experience a kind of self-efficacy—that is, they are able to influence the environment through their own behavior. Being an active participant in interaction with the environment, new objects, or a person stimulates problem-solving behavior, and develops the motivation to deal with new things. I believe that you should consciously encourage this behavior in horses when you train them. We humans are obviously concerned with steering the horse's activity in the direction that makes sense for us and the horse in training. An example would be, when getting the horse used to a new halter, rewarding him as soon as he approaches this object, or even stretches his nose in the direction of the halter noseband.

After Mona has tolerated the halter being in contact with her head for a few seconds, I reach under her throatlatch and lift the end of the poll strap along the off side of her head with my hand. She still isn't sure about my hand being on her head, but she accepts it. I don't want to overwhelm her, so I lower my hand again. I repeat this movement until Mona stops finding it threatening. Only then do I slowly place the strap across her poll behind her ears. When I can calmly fasten the buckle on my side of her head, I praise her with my voice. Then, I take the halter off again, and she can finally stand in her stall without one!

HER OWN SPACE
The Stall

Mona still isn't sure about me approaching her in the stall, and changes her expression and flattens her ears as I do. I understand that she sees the stall as her space. We mostly only see our domesticated horses defending their stall in connection with feeding time. Feeding time is often one of the few highlights of their otherwise rather monotonous day. This behavior can also be learned aggression toward other horses or the handler. The behavior has been learned because it maybe occurred at random to begin with, but was then rewarded because the horse was subsequently given food.

It is very interesting to observe that a Mustang mare is quicker to react with defensive behavior when she is in a restricted area. If she is approached in the stall but also when she is led to the wall where the horses are tied up, her escape route is limited. The more freely I work with her, the more tolerant she is of my approach. In turn, this shows me that my preferred approach with young horses—showing them new things in the round pen or arena—is right.

Why Horses Equate Restriction with Threat

A horse's reaction to something unfamiliar appears to be closely linked to his ability to flee. If a horse is prevented from the outset from using flight to escape from a new situation, he will tend to use defense from the beginning. The behavior of the Mustang mare shows this very clearly from the outset, and we should also take account of it in our domesticated horses. Defensive reactions no longer play such a major role in their behavioral repertoire, but just "letting things wash over them" could also have negative consequences for their mental state. Making the horse feel helpless or taking away his ability to flee never seems to be the right way: we could quickly exploit "learned helplessness" and immediately nip in the bud any motivation to interact with us in a positive manner.

THE FIRST MONTH

1	2	3	4	5	6	
8	9	10	11	12	13	14
15	16	17	18	19	20	21
22	23	24	25	26	27	28
29	30	31				

THE SECOND MONTH

			1	2	3	4
5	6	7	8	9	10	11
12	13	14	15	16	17	18
19	20	21	22	23	24	25
26	27	28	29	30		

THE THIRD MONTH

					1	2
3	4	5	6	7	8	9
10	11	12	13	14	15	16
17	18	19	20	21	22	23
24	25	26	27	28	29	30
31						

I don't want to trick Mona into having her bridle put on. The mare should understand each individual step. You can see that she isn't able to relax, but she accepts it calmly.

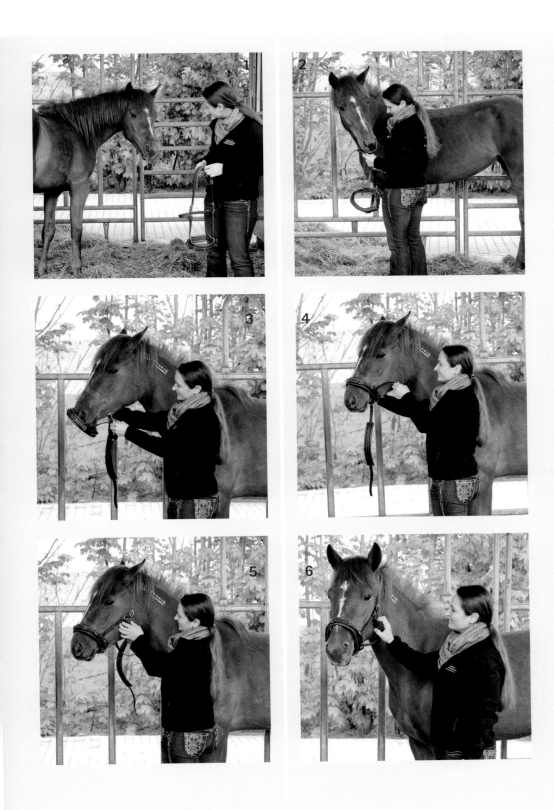

Before I go into the round pen with Mona today, I get her to stand in our tying area for a short while. I have already done this repeatedly in recent days. I want her to gradually become used to being groomed until it becomes part of her routine. I don't tie Mona up yet, but pull the rope through the tying ring, and stroke her neck and back a little with my hand. I want her to see the lead rope going in the direction of the wall, but not have her freedom of movement restricted by it. I take her away from this area after a short time. I have the impression that the boundary to the front makes her feel hemmed in, and I don't want to expose her to this feeling for too long. We continue in the direction of the round pen. Before we start training, I allow her to eat a little grass, which she gratefully accepts.

I always follow a similar pattern in the round pen. She can move around me at liberty in walk to begin with, and then in trot and canter. Moving forward still isn't her favorite thing. What she really likes is to come into me and have a break! I then get Mona to yield her forehand and hindquarters a few times. Having a familiar sequence to follow, before adding anything new to the agenda, gives her stability and security.

Today, I want to feel my way farther toward her hindquarters and picking up her back feet. I have a fair amount of respect for her hindquarters. During these first days with Mona, I have noticed that things she perceives from behind are especially likely to elicit a sudden startle response. When she gets a fright, she violently jumps and leaps away. It isn't like the flight that I have seen in other young horses. They run away for a short distance, making them easier to predict than the Mustang mare.

Her sudden and violent reactions mean that I have to be more careful when training her hindquarters than I would with other horses. I stroke her hindquarters down toward her leg and notice that her ears go back and that her attention is on each of my movements. I try to keep standing straight, and not to have my head and upper body in the "strike range" of her hindquarters.

The first time I get to her hock, she gives a sudden defensive reaction in the form of a kick, in a short, fast arc back and to the side! I was right to be cautious. After the kick, Mona immediately stands quietly again. Like a rapid reflex, the brief moment of violence is over. I stroke her leg with regular movements from the top down, inch by inch. Just before I reach her hock, I praise Mona and take a step back. I give her a little food reward that she enjoys. She is very attentive after her treat and grasps very quickly that standing still is probably what brings her a reward. After a few repetitions, I am actually able to stroke her hind leg all the way down to her cannon bone—phew!

I begin the same game on the other side. Her full focus is on me, and she doesn't let me out of her sight for one second. When I manage it on the other side, too, I get her to walk forward a little, to ease the tension.

I then do the relaxation exercise that I have been doing with her for a few moments in recent days. She no longer shakes her head like she did at first. Mona understood incredibly quickly how to relieve the pressure—by lowering her head.

THE FIRST GIRTHING EXERCISE

To get a horse used to something being in contact with him around his barrel, I use a soft lunge line. I carefully place it around the horse's barrel so that I can immediately remove it if I need to. As I have already described, I don't want to ambush the horse with anything and force him to endure pressure that he finds unpleasant. This breach of trust would only cause problems in our subsequent work together.

For the first girthing exercise, it is important that the horse calmly accepts being touched on the sides of his belly, as well as underneath, and between and behind his front legs. If this is done too quickly or in too much of a rush and the horse remembers it as a negative experience, it can trigger problems with girthing up or saddling later on.

I start by putting the rope loosely over Mona's back. As a preliminary exercise, I gently swing the rope sideways against her belly with my hand. With my other hand, I encourage the mare to lower her head by giving gentle pulses on the lead rope. I stop swinging the rope as soon as she lowers her head.

The low head carriage encourages the horse to relax both her mind and the muscles in her body. You can see by looking at Mona's facial expression that her eyes and mouth are relaxed. Conditioning this posture not only encourages relaxation but also gives the horse a "say."

This conditioning motivates Mona to actively cooperate by lowering her head when exposed to new, slightly "annoying" stimuli, such as the gentle flapping of the rope. I repeat this preliminary exercise with her a few times (I actually no longer need to help her lower her head by giving her impulses—she does it by herself!) This is a great moment because I realize she is communicating directly with me. This is the interaction I want because it feels like we are talking to each other.

The Stop Signal

If you teach a horse to lower his head by using and then removing a stimulus that he initially finds unpleasant (by definition: negative reinforcement), lowering the head can become an indicator of something unpleasant. This gives the horse a "say" in new and unfamiliar situations that might be unpleasant at first—such as doing up the girth for the first time. This reinforces the self-efficacy I described earlier (see p. 27), and motivates the horse to contribute his own solution to the situation. Since lowering the head also triggers a relaxed posture, you can gradually increase the stimulus and the horse will accept it more and more.

We have now reached the point where I can carefully take the rope under the belly, from one side to the other. It must feel strange for a Mustang to be encircled by a rope for the first time. In the wild, it could mean danger or even death. The preliminary work that we have done is all the more important so the horse knows how to deal with these risky situations.

I take one end of the rope in each hand and build up tentative pressure in gentle impulses. The benefit of creating a new stimulus using impulses has the advantage that the horse quickly becomes habituated as the pressure intensifies and then abates again monotonously. I can steadily slightly increase the intensity of the pressure then reduce it again after about a second. Working in this way does not put any physical or mental pressure on the horse. The horse should learn that the pressure always eases off. This, subconsciously, results in habituation. The organism learns to increasingly fade out the stimulus since the stimulus is not relevant to it. This is precisely how you want the horse to respond to this type of pressure: neither a defensive reaction on a physical level, nor a stress response on an emotional level. To later be able to securely fasten the girth, you want the horse to accept something being around his body, and no longer perceive it as something dangerous or unpleasant.

Mona's body language is very expressive, and she clearly shows what she does and doesn't like. Will she show that she doesn't like

THE FIRST MONTH

1	2	3	4	5	6	7
8	9	10	11	12	13	14
15	16	17	18	19	20	21
22	23	24	25	26	27	28
29	30	31				

THE SECOND MONTH

			1	2	3	4
5	6	7	8	9	10	11
12	13	14	15	16	17	18
19	20	21	22	23	24	25
26	27	28	29	30		

THE THIRD MONTH

					1	2
3	4	5	6	7	8	9
10	11	12	13	14	15	16
17	18	19	20	21	22	23
24	25	26	27	28	29	30
31						

something being around her body? As it turns out, the preparatory work has paid off. She communicates clearly because she lowers her head after a few cautious impulses, and I immediately release the rope. The stop signal works. I now know that she isn't quite comfortable with pressure building up around her belly, but I let her cooperate with me and have a say in the decision first. Lowering her head also causes Mona to relax her back and abdominal muscles, to keep breathing and not to adopt a defensive posture in the first place—even if defense in this case takes the form of going rigid. This is often seen in horses that have not been calmly shown girthing and, later, saddling. These horses stop breathing and tense their entire body when the girth is done up.

Low head carriage makes a positive contribution to a relaxed basic attitude—physically as well as mentally. With Mona, I can, therefore, gradually slightly intensify the pressure with every impulse, just as a matter of course. I release the pressure as soon as she gives her answer. Some people might think that you will never be able to tighten the girth if you keep releasing the pressure, but that is not the case, because the horse's acceptance keeps increasing, as does the stimulus threshold where Mona lowers her head. This is because of the subconscious habituation that is taking place. I maintain the pressure for a fraction of a second longer each time until, within a period of 30 seconds, I can actually wrap the rope around her pretty tightly for a few seconds. She now keeps her head in the low position the whole time. For that reason, there is never any tension in this situation, and we can finish the girthing exercise after a few minutes.

THE SEVENTH DAY

Don't Take Anything for Granted: Entering a Space

The first week with my Mustang mare has now come to an end. I am astonished to discover all the things she is willing to do with me. I haven't needed to ambush her with anything. She is incredibly quick on the uptake, so some steps don't take long at all, and I have seen some great progress in this short time.

But, on the other hand, I can clearly see what bothers her—things that we take for granted with our domesticated horses. We "fiddle around" with our horses when they are in their retreat—the stall. We put halters on their heads no matter whether they are eating, taking a nap, or have something entirely different in mind, and we work with them at whatever time of day. We lead them into narrow, dark passageways where there are hardly any options for escape, then tie them to walls so that their view of their surroundings almost entirely disappears.

Mona's paddock stall is outdoors. I take my time leading her into our barn aisle for the first time. To begin with, she finds entering a "room"—four walls that only allow limited visibility—anything but easy. Our aisle is slightly higher up than the outdoor area and is accessed via a slightly sloping concrete ramp. During the day, it is also slightly darker in the barn than it is outside. I lead Mona in the direction of the large entrance. I walk slightly ahead of her and take the first step into the barn. Mona is right behind me, but she stops as soon as she sets foot in the aisle. She looks into the room, but doesn't move. She doesn't see any good reason for going into this place that she can't see properly. There are other horses in the aisle and

Being able to see what's going on around them is an important safety factor for horses. As long as his movement isn't restricted, a horse always has the option of running away.

she notices them, but they aren't enough reason for her to enter the building. Mona pulls slightly on the halter and leans backward and away from me. I calmly resist. She is familiar with the principle from our work in the round pen—I will not yield to her backward pressure. Just a few seconds later, she releases the pressure in my direction. I calmly breathe in and out and just keep standing a few steps ahead of her on the ramp. I talk to her in a relaxed voice. After a short while, I start to give gentle impulses on the halter. She actually plucks up her courage, walks up the ramp, and stands in our grooming area. We don't consider this area to be cramped, because three horses could stand next to each other comfortably. It becomes clear to me again that we often see things very differently to how horses see them!

As Mona comes behind me, I can tell that she is walking apprehensively. She looks as if she is walking over an unfamiliar surface for the first time. I realize how unpleasant this situation is for her. There is enough space in the grooming area to calmly turn the horse around. I give Mona a food reward and lead her straight out of the barn. Her relief is palpable!

How Buildings Interfere with the Horse's Nature

For us, having buildings, rooms, and walls around us means we feel protected. Other species also see caves and narrow passageways as their home, just as we sought refuge in caves in prehistoric times. Horses are designed for the open steppe and protection to them means being able to keep watch over the open space. They depend on being able to spot dangers lurking in the distance and being able to flee in time or defend themselves with a well-aimed kick.

Depriving horses of their ability to see around them by taking them into buildings goes against their nature. They lose the ability to keep watch over the area and to take flight.

An incredible relationship is developing over such a short time.

WEEK 2

To prepare the mare for her new life, I do more work on her "life skills" in the second week. Tying up, grooming, and possibly riding will, I hope, be normal for her at some point.

After just one week with Mona, I notice myself thinking more and more often about my attitude, how I handle horses, my own actions, and how I see the world of horses, and I look at some things differently.

I am becoming increasingly aware that horses must have a very different way of looking at things that I have long taken for granted. This is clear from the Mustang's natural attitude.

The new "first" encounters are, therefore, something very special, and I am grateful

the horse accepts them and trusts me. On the other hand, she also naturally takes some things in stride. For example, she starts to see me as a kind of substitute horse or, even better, as a leader and attachment figure, within the first few days. This becomes clear in the round pen where, when we are working, her focus is solely on me. Even when the herd in the pen next to us starts acting up, Mona only has eyes for me.

THE ABILITY TO CONCENTRATE

Science has not yet been able to say how many minutes horses can concentrate. It has been established that they are probably not able to concentrate for as long as

30 or even 60 minutes at a time. It is vital that horses are able to quickly direct their attention to possible danger. In communication with people, it is, therefore, all the more important that we train and improve their focus on us minute by minute. This shifts the focus from threatening external stimuli to our signals that, in the best case, motivate the horse to pay more and more attention to us.

THE TYING AREA

The outside wall, where I tie up horses to groom them, is still difficult. It is out in the open, but the area is covered.

Mona feels hemmed in here. She responds to my touch quite differently than she did when interacting freely in the round pen. I obviously don't tie her up here properly yet, but just pull the long lead rope through the ring. I keep giving her pulses on the rope so that she realizes that here, too, the forward pressure releases as soon as she yields to it. By doing this, I want to prevent her from ever unintentionally exerting pressure on her poll and then not knowing how to deal with it.

The outdoor grooming area might seem spacious and open to us, but to Mona, it means that her escape is restricted. We shouldn't take it for granted that we can tie up a flight animal to a wall, even if it becomes a matter of course at some point.

Tying

We need to understand that approaching a wall when the halter exerts pressure on the sensitive poll seems illogical to the horse. The logical flight path in response to confusing and dangerous situations would always be into the open. By tying them to a wall, we deprive horses of this option. For that reason, it is advisable to show them this step by step, and to be very cautious and calm about it.

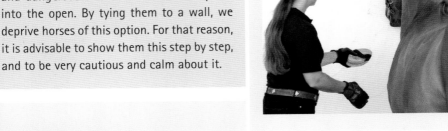

THE FIRST BRUSH

Today, I want to familiarize Mona with a grooming brush. For a long time, Mona has taken care of her own coat by rolling in sandy soil or by contact with other horses. As a future riding horse, grooming will be part of her daily routine.

I start by letting her sniff the brush, and she explores it with gentle nibbles. She seems very interested in the smell—after all, the brush does smell like another horse. Then, I touch her coat with the brush for the first time, which is a special moment for me. It feels as if I am officially taking her into my care. Feeding, grooming, and protection—these are the areas of responsibility every horse owner needs to take care of, along with riding.

THE CHALLENGE: PICKING UP THE FEET

This week, I want to continue getting Mona used to having her feet picked up. I can't put off the appointment with the farrier much longer. Mona's hooves seem sturdy and hard and they appear to be at a good angle to her leg, but the front ones look as if they need work soon.

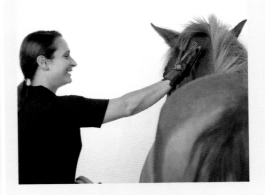

The first touch with a brush! Mona is allowed to sniff the new object first. After her initial apprehension, she finally allows the contact.

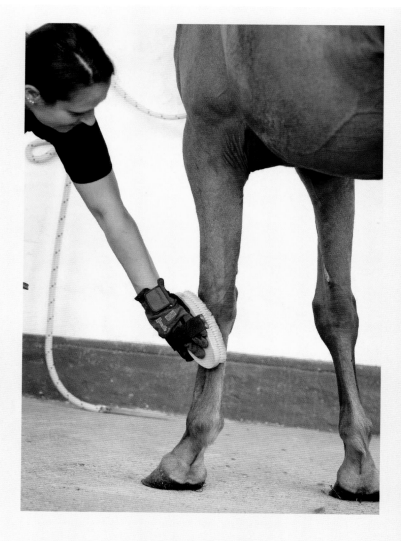

I follow a similar sequence every day. The mare now approaches me curiously when I go up to her paddock stall, and sweetly allows me to put on her halter. I still have to be a little careful with my movements at her head. I consciously keep my posture passive—slightly turned away from her—as I approach. I always let her come slightly toward me of her own accord before putting on the halter. I then take her to the outdoor grooming area and get her to stand by the tying ring. I just pull the rope loosely through the ring. She accepts the brush well. She already seems to find the brush strokes enjoyable in some areas. She stretches her head up luxuriantly when I scratch the underside of her neck. I can now stroke her legs with the soft brush more and more, and I can also touch her hind legs all the way down to her hooves.

Her reactions at her hindquarters are still sudden and very violent. I decide not to practice picking up her back feet at the tying ring any more, but in her "happy place"—the round pen.

I stroke her hindquarters with a soft lunge line and let it swing gently against her legs. Mona no longer thinks this is bad, and I can desensitize her to the recurring touch, in a relaxed upright position. If I do it like this, my head is nowhere near her lightning-fast hindquarters. The mare stands very calmly as I work and realizes that what I'm doing is not associated with any pressure or directly being held. I swing the lunge line so that there is an open loop around one of her hind legs. Then, I hold firmly onto the rope with both hands and very gently touch Mona's pastern with it. She finds it strange and takes a few quick steps back. What's good about this method is that the contact that she initially wants to get rid of remains and the rope loosens as soon as she stands still, because it is an open loop. If Mona really wants to run away or if she panics, the rope will loosen completely, so she won't become tangled up. The brief moment of backward movement is over again just a few seconds later, and I can start building up a little tension with the lunge line and immediately releasing it again. After a few repetitions, I can build up much more tension. My aim is for her to lift up her hoof easily and to allow the loop to support it, as if it were my hand. She shouldn't fend off my hand later, but trustingly give me her hoof.

Mona now stands quietly and accepts the lunge line touching her from her hoof to her hock.

Mona is getting better and better at lifting up her front feet, but the back ones are more critical. In the round pen, the mare doesn't feel as restricted as she does at the tying ring.

This is a critical moment because I want her to lift her hoof up from the ground without immediately kicking out. I stand next to her shoulder, outside the kick zone, and give slightly more intensive pulses on the loop around her fetlock. I accompany the pulses on the lunge line with the voice command "foot." The challenge for Mona, now, is to understand what I want. I intensify the pulses for a moment and she briefly lifts her foot from the floor. I immediately release the rope and give her a food reward. Mona cooperates actively if she is expecting a food reward. I want to immediately associate this important thing with something positive. I repeat my strategy: pulse on the rope and voice command—and, sure enough, she slightly lifts her foot again. I am relieved to have managed this first step.

This exercise is part of our basic program for the coming days, and I manage more and more often to get her to let the rope support her when she lifts her leg. I vary the exercise slightly. Between times, I want Mona to keep her foot on the ground while I stroke her leg with my hand. I praise her soothingly as I do it. Another time I give the command, "Foot." She should feel certain about what I want from her and what will immediately be praised.

For the next step, I stand by her hindquarters. I don't take hold of her leg at the pastern yet, because this could trigger another massive defensive reaction. I place her leg in the lunge line next to mine, gradually building up more and more direct contact. Step by step, I am able to get her to put her leg next to my thigh.

DAILY MUCKING OUT
A Threat?

When we muck out our paddock stalls, we send the horses out into the paddock area. The advantage of this is that we don't expose the horses to dust when we shake out the straw. If I use body language and a stern gaze, Mona sees being sent out to the paddock from her area as a threat, so I have chosen a ritual to keep the interaction between my trainees and the Mustang mare as stress-free as possible. She gets a small portion of hay in the paddock when we are mucking out, and the paddock is blocked off with a rope. Over time, Mona has internalized this ritual and goes to her paddock area as soon as she sees the wheelbarrow. The process gives her security and she doesn't think the intrusion into "her" stall is all that bad after all. She calmly turns around in the paddock and watches me muck out. This simple, but clear rule is not "discussed." The horse learns not to use aggressive behavior as a way of getting something positive, be that space or food.

THE FIRST MONTH

1	2	3	4	5	6	7
8	9	10	11	12	13	14
15	16	17	18	19	20	21
22	23	24	25	26	27	28
29	30	31				

THE SECOND MONTH

		1	2	3	4
5	6	7	8	9	10	11
12	13	14	15	16	17	18
19	20	21	22	23	24	25
26	27	28	29	30		

THE THIRD MONTH

				1	2
3	4	5	6	7	8	9
10	11	12	13	14	15	16
17	18	19	20	21	22	23
24	25	26	27	28	29	30
31						

40

FIRST SUPPLING EXERCISES

I want to increasingly transform liberty work with Mona into valuable suppling work. She already trots and canters around me well in the round pen, but I need to keep up my body tension to prevent her from falling straight back into a slower gait. She is incredibly attentive to my body language. She is getting better and better at adopting a long-and-low outline in trot of her own accord. Using body tension and exhalation alone, I create a rewarding effect, where I allow Mona to keep coming back to walk—that's her biggest reward! I am always astounded by what this animal naturally perceives and by how subtly I need to communicate to do her justice.

I am now starting to lunge her in the cavesson for minutes at a time. If she lowers

Introducing Rituals for Security

It's like with people—knowing how something works makes us feel secure. Horses are exactly the same. Whether it's daily mucking out or the sequence of a training session, the horse knows what happens next and can prepare for it. However, if everyday life is always the same, there is a risk that boredom will set in or that horses will start to anticipate things. Routine is important, but variety and novelty foster curiosity and motivate the horse to look for solutions to new problems or exercises himself, which maintains the self-efficacy I have already talked about (see p. 27). The right balance between security from clear and familiar sequences, and variety to encourage concentration and attention, is clearly the key to good training.

You can condition a gymnastically beneficial outline during work at liberty by rewarding the horse the moment he shows the desired posture, by lowering your own body tension.

This is how Mona has learned to keep returning to the long-and-low outline.

her head and trots nice and low for a few strides, she can immediately come back to walk. I then let her raise her head slightly for a brief sequence. She should carry her own head for a moment through slight muscular tension and fine flexibility in the poll. To get her to do this, I raise the hand that is holding the lunge line and slightly increase the basic tension in my body—again, just for a few seconds—and then another transition to walk. Mona responds well to this kind of praise and tries to follow the signals correctly. This is a good start to suppling work.

Short, Rewarding Sequences for Effective Learning

Short learning sequences where the horse responds to a signal, such as a change in body tension, for example, immediately followed by something positive, actively encourage learning and motivation. The horse also learns that it is beneficial to pay attention and respond to the human giving the signal.

THE FIRST GROUND POLE EXERCISE

As part of our further suppling work and to improve concentration, I keep getting Mona to move her forehand and hindquarters and to take a few steps sideways. Today, I have put a natural-colored wooden pole in the round pen. I don't think that walking over it will be too difficult for a horse born in the wild.

Mona, on the other hand, thinks it makes more sense to walk around the pole because there is enough space at the side. She's right! In an emergency, maneuvering around an obstacle conserves more energy than getting over it. Mona isn't really scared of the wooden pole; she just doesn't see any point in stepping over it.

I use the rope to guide her more precisely to the middle, and after a quick look down at it, she walks over the pole. I reinforce this with verbal praise so she understands what I want.

THE FIRST MONTH

1	2	3	4	5	6	7
8	9	10	11	12	13	14
15	16	17	18	19	20	21
22	23	24	25	26	27	28
29	30	31				

THE SECOND MONTH

		1	2	3	4
5	6	7	8	9	10	11
12	13	14	15	16	17	18
19	20	21	22	23	24	25
26	27	28	29	30		

THE THIRD MONTH

					1	2
3	4	5	6	7	8	9
10	11	12	13	14	15	16
17	18	19	20	21	22	23
24	25	26	27	28	29	30
31						

If we think about it, we often take for granted the things that we expect from our horses. Many of these things make no sense to them. We should always keep in mind that horses would deal with situations completely differently in the wild. Often people even punish horses for the solutions they find. The art of good communication and horse-friendly training is to guide (in the truest sense of the word) the horse to the solution that fits with ours. It is important for the horse to realize that trying to find a solution is rewarding, so we encourage active participation and solution-finding.

A horse has no idea that walking over poles is important for his physical fitness. He has even less of a clue that a certain head and neck carriage and active hindquarters will help him to carry a rider. We often see good solutions in horses' behavior that are worth encouraging. Our training needs to

You can tell the mare is a quick learner by her alert expression. Things need to make sense to her before she will engage with them. This alertness and the motivation to find solutions should always be encouraged.

43

be flexible for this: it could mean maybe continuing with something that you didn't even want to be doing with the horse at that moment.

When dealing with the Mustang mare, she clearly shows that she wants to find solutions herself. She wants to actively tackle new situations, rather than just waiting or putting up with something. It's obviously hard to say whether this is a genetic predisposition or something that was trained during the first years of her life. I often see inactivity or even introversion in our domesticated horses, which is certainly a learned behavior, and in some cases could even be "learned helplessness." Learned helplessness is where the animal has learned that he can't independently "escape" some situations, so he chooses to be passive by tolerating and enduring negative stimuli and an aversive environment.

It is really no surprise that horses like this tend to be inactive or even withdrawn in new situations. I think that we should always encourage horses to cooperate actively and keep asking them new questions where they can and are allowed to find a solution!

SADDLE PAD AND GIRTH

Today, I want to try putting a saddle pad and a lungeing roller on Mona for the first time. I start with exercises she is familiar with. I want the familiar routine to give her security and get her to focus on me. I have already given her an idea of what I want from her with the preliminary exercise where I put the rope around her belly so I do the same with the lungeing roller, but without the saddle pad to begin with. I stroke her body with this object. The rings on the lungeing roller jingle a little. After stroking Mona's side and her saddle area a few times, I put the lungeing roller over her back. She pays close attention to what I'm doing and listens intently to me behind her. The situation is completely different to the familiar rope. I talk to her quietly and get her to lower her head slightly and, at that moment, take the roller off her back. I walk a few steps with her to show her that there is always a solution and again, something familiar ends with peace and relaxation. I repeat this process a few times.

The next step is to get her to stand quietly while I reach under her belly to take hold of the other end of the roller. I don't want to do up the girth right away, because who knows how she will react when the pressure doesn't release. I bring the ends of the girth together and release them again. Then I bring them together again and so on. It's the same as the rope exercise that she has already learned. She lowers her head again and holds it in a relaxed position. I am astounded that she transfers the solution from the rope to the girth, because the

THE FIRST MONTH

1 2 3 4 5 6 **7**
8 9 10 11 12 13 14
15 16 17 18 19 20 **21**
22 23 24 25 26 27 **28**
29 30 31

THE SECOND MONTH

          1 2 3 **4**
5 6 7 8 9 10 **11**
12 13 14 15 16 17 **18**
19 20 21 22 23 24 **25**
26 27 28 29 30

THE THIRD MONTH

                1 **2**
3 4 5 6 7 8 **9**
10 11 12 13 14 15 **16**
17 18 19 20 21 22 **23**
24 25 26 27 28 29 **30**
31

girth feels completely different. I don't have the feeling that she would overreact if I did up the girth, because her body is relaxed. She is listening attentively behind her, but apparently not fearing anything terrible.

I do up the girth, obviously not too tightly, but so that it won't slip if she suddenly reacts. The next big step is to move her forward with this thing on her. I know young horses that react defensively or, in the worst case, with panic, when they feel that something is restricting them as they move. I try to walk in front of Mona very calmly and matter-of-factly, and she actually follows me for a few steps. I stand and praise her—she doesn't overreact—we've taken a big step!

Habituation to the saddle pad is a different matter altogether, even though I have just shown Mona how girthing works. The next challenge will be to tolerate something bigger on her back that also moves. For that reason, I won't start getting her used to and preparing her for saddling by putting a saddle on her back. I would have to do up the girth of a saddle, properly and immediately, to stop anything from going wrong.

The pad is different to a plastic bag that I can fold out bit by bit, but I follow a very similar procedure with it. I stand calmly next to Mona and let the rope hang loosely. I stroke first her side and then her back with the folded pad using big, repetitive movements. The pad isn't completely over her back yet, just on one side. I then stroke her with it from front to back, open up the pad while I am doing so, and let it slide over her back.

I also use relaxation as a reward for habituation to the saddle pad.

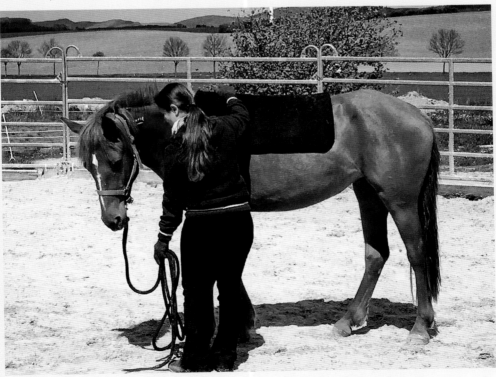

Building up the exercises in logical steps protects you and the horse from overreaction.

I make big movements with the pad and slide it back and forth on Mona's back. I then lift it up a few inches and let it gently fall back onto her back. My movements are very matter of fact, but careful. The mare should realize that nothing bad happens, even if the thing moves back and forth on her back.

To encourage her to accept the object, I no longer reward her by completely removing the pad from her back as soon as she relaxes and lowers her head. The reward is now that the pad stays still.

We do the exercise for one or two minutes. I then "release" Mona, and remove the pad from her back. Then we do another few circuits in walk. The process is always the same for her, even if I am familiarizing her with a new object. Always following the same process gives her the security I mentioned earlier.

In the next training session, I put the pad on her back and pat it with my hand. Mona thinks this is very strange. Her expression changes and she turns her head in my direction. Whenever she does that and tenses her lips, she is showing that she finds the stimulus unpleasant and wants to get rid of it. At this moment, I don't just keep patting harder and let her tolerate the unpleasant situation, but stick with the same intensity. I want to encourage her to come up with a new solution, because defensive behavior and wanting to nip are not the right ones. I help her to relax and lower her head again. She accepts this willingly, and I immediately stop "annoying" her with the patting.

It would be wrong to punish Mona's defensive behavior by hitting her nose, for example, when she is just honestly showing that something isn't right for her. You see this kind of behavior from people far too often. Even if it is sometimes difficult, you have to ignore a horse's unpleasant behavior in some situations and, at the same time, try to show him a better path.

Once I have shown Mona that the pad on her back isn't dangerous, even if it moves, I walk a few steps with her. Even now she is still calm! I praise Mona, then halt again, walk on again, and halt again. During this exercise, I am again astounded by how calm this Mustang is. I am happy that my preparatory work has led to this result.

Discovering the world together brings us closer. Arousing curiosity and discovering something positive strengthens the bond.

WEEK 3

MAKING TRAINING POSITIVE

After achieving such a big step yesterday, I want to do something more fun with Mona today, where she doesn't have to "tolerate" any new objects. I want to keep her training varied and for her to always feel that time with me is something positive. It's nice to see that she approaches me alertly and curiously whenever I walk past her paddock. When I take her with me, she seems to be waiting to experience something new.

Today, I want to try a preliminary exercise for mounting, which involves teaching the young horse to approach me sideways. Once a horse has understood this, you can even get him to do it from the mounting block. You will then have a horse that cooperates when being mounted. If mounting has negative connotations for your horse, he will be tense and you might even end up carrying the mounting block around after him.

This exercise is based on operant conditioning and the principle of trial and error. I must turn off my influence as soon as the mare takes one small step in with her hindquarters. I lean my upper body back slightly to explain to the horse that the solution lies in coming in toward me.

LATERAL MOVEMENT TOWARD ME

I train lateral movement toward me by rewarding a chance reaction. This is operant conditioning in action. For this exercise, it can be helpful to stand the horse facing a boundary, such as the arena fence. Position yourself so that you can move backward to give the horse space. I tend to lean back slightly with my upper body. I start by slowly directing my gaze toward the point where the lateral movement will begin (this is where your leg driving the lateral movement will be when you are in the saddle) and intensifying the pressure. I like to work with a stick or a whip with a lash. Horses sometimes respond to my signal by moving away from the pressure toward the fence. However, if you have already worked on exercises involving sending the horse away and drawing him back toward you, he will quickly find the right solution. The first correct response begins with one inward step with the hindquarters. At precisely this moment, it is essential that you remove the pressure and praise the horse, lower your body tension, and take a short break.

I have found that this mare moves toward me very willingly and sometimes even increases the pace as she does so. I introduce this exercise next to the fence of the round pen. She finds the correct solution within a few moments and moves her hindquarters half a step toward me. You have to watch very closely for this moment. It must immediately be clear to the horse that there is a way to relieve this pressure. He must not be kept under pressure for too long, as this causes unnecessary stress. If the horse has previously learned in respect exercises to move away from pressure from the handler, it might at first seem illogical to be allowed to approach a human. The horse has to rethink the situation. He must want to "escape" the pressure, but needs to pay close attention to the handler's body language to see which direction of movement will achieve this.

I give Mona a short break after her first successful attempt, and then repeat the exercise three or four times. I want her to make the connection between the signal I am giving with my posture, my gaze, and the resulting pressure directed toward her belly, and this movement. Horses always seem to find this exercise quite complicated, which makes it all the more astounding that they so quickly learn to make this association, if we communicate it correctly—that is, with the right intensity and timing.

In this exercise, pressure doesn't necessarily mean touching the horse. I would only touch him if he absolutely will not move from his position. If the horse isn't showing any signs of figuring it out, I would start by lightly touching his belly. I don't need to touch Mona at all. I am sure that, because of the exercises that I have done with her so far, she knows that I will reinforce any attempt she makes to find a solution. She will most likely offer a solution that I will then promptly praise.

Mona is gradually developing more strength and energy. She tells me this every so often with a few exuberant bucks!

Even if she doesn't offer me any lateral movement yet, the idea and the beginnings of this movement will be there after a few repetitions. For that reason, we finish this exercise and move onto something completely different. This clears both our heads after this slightly more complicated exercise.

I get Mona to relax again by sending her forward in trot and canter. I can see how much she benefits from moving away from this intensely focused task and onto some moderate exercise. When she moves forward now, she more often tends to throw in a few happy bucks and leaps, which I never saw her do before. In this context, I don't see this behavior as negative. It's quite the opposite, in fact, as being able to let off steam and get rid of any tension in the body is a relief for the horse. It's very important that you always allow your horse to enjoy this time.

Distinguishing Between Sending Away and Inviting In

Horses can differentiate between the subtlest body language signals. For communication in the herd, it is important that every horse pays attention to the other horses' signals, not just to keep the herd in sync, but to communicate directly with each other. Horses use gestures, facial expressions, and body tension to signal whether another horse should move away or approach them. It is important in the herd for horses to be able to send each other away. However, for cohesion in the herd, it is equally important to be able to invite another horse in— for positive social interaction such as mutual grooming, for example.

WORKING WITH DIFFERENT OBJECTS

Cones

Today, I put out some cones for the first time. Mona hasn't seen these banded plastic cones before. I place them every 6 feet or so in the middle of the round pen. Mona is curious and examines the soft obstacles. I keep doing groundwork with her on the long rope, vary the distance to the cones, and also work her between them. They are still quite far apart so she doesn't feel hemmed in. After a few minutes, I move them closer and closer together. When the cones are about 3 feet apart, she peers down at them and quickens her pace slightly as she walks between them. I get her to walk through this narrow gap two or three times until she realizes that it isn't dangerous for her.

Poles

There are some colored poles behind the barrier of the round pen. I bring a pole into the work area to go with the cones. She has already seen a wooden pole, but this one has a colorful plastic cover. Mona quickly applies what she has already learned and realizes that I praise her as soon as she walks over the pole. I begin to incorporate the command "Over" every time she walks over the pole. I say the word just before she gets to the pole and reward her immediately after she has stepped over it by bringing her into me and giving her a small food reward. After a few repetitions, she knows that she not only gets verbal praise for walking over the pole, but also a food reward. She is now very motivated and you can even see it in her face. Associating walking over the pole with a command has the advantage that I will later be able to send her over it at liberty and at faster gaits.

THE FIRST MONTH

1	2	3	4	5	6	**7**
8	9	10	11	12	13	**14**
15	16	17	18	19	20	21
22	23	24	25	26	27	**28**
29	30	31				

THE SECOND MONTH

			1	2	3	**4**
5	6	7	8	9	10	**11**
12	13	14	15	16	17	**18**
19	20	21	22	23	24	**25**
26	27	28	29	30		

THE THIRD MONTH

					1	2
3	4	5	6	7	8	9
10	11	12	13	14	15	**16**
17	18	19	20	21	22	**23**
24	25	26	27	28	29	**30**
31						

Concentration During Training

In our stressful everyday lives, we often find it difficult to concentrate, and to focus on the horse we are working with. Concentration is essential if you are really going to be able to communicate precisely and subtly with an animal as sensitive as a horse. When working with the Mustang mare, I have realized that, if I don't concentrate and have my mind fully on the job, she could react violently. I can't give precise signals if my mind is elsewhere. You can't just give a signal any old how and expect a precise answer from the horse. When my aids are vague then I can only expect vague answers to them. When dealing with Mona, I can really see how clearly horses expect, and also show, intention among themselves. They are focused on their next move, while we are often preoccupied with the past or the future, which prevents us from concentrating on the present moment. Horses must find this unnatural, strange, or even threatening.

I find that when I am working with Mona and I have another appointment afterward or I somehow feel under time pressure, many things just don't work at all, and she even reacts defensively to touch. For that reason, I do our training sessions at the end of the day when I am relaxed, and I don't set a specific time limit in which I have to achieve something, so my work with her feels much freer and more focused.

"PARKING" AT THE MOUNTING BLOCK

Today, Mona and I are repeating the lateral-movement-toward-me exercise. My aim is for her to play an active role when I want to mount and not just allow it to happen to her, which is why I will later use this exercise for "parking" at the mounting block. Even if she "parks" in response to a specific command, the horse is actively cooperating in the process of mounting. From a psychological point of view, this is completely different to passively tolerating something. It gives you the opportunity to praise the horse for this part of the mounting process, because, let's be honest, being mounted itself isn't really rewarding for the horse!

We begin the lateral exercise at the boundary to the round pen again. The lungeing roller and the pad are already hanging on the fence. I want to gradually incorporate these objects more and more into Mona's everyday life. I would like to work with her with the pad and lungeing roller for a few minutes later during this session. I have also put out a mounting block—not because I want to get on her back today, but because I want to show Mona that a person being higher up than she is isn't anything to be afraid of.

The mounting block is in the middle as I work on the lateral exercise with her at the edge of the round pen. Integrating a new object into training shouldn't be anything special for her. Because I do not behave any differently in the presence of this object, she should just accept it.

Today, I manage to get her to take one or two steps toward me in succession. I am astonished by how much she has progressed after just a few repetitions.

The first time I lean over her from the mounting block, Mona listens behind with interest and tolerates my touch over her back.

Again, I realize how important it is that I focus fully on the training. If I exert pressure for too long and perhaps too distinctly, Mona's body tension instantly changes. Her facial expression becomes tense and she quickly makes a threatening face with her ears pinned back. I don't take it too seriously and try to stick to my routine and not let it bother me.

I am working with Mona on the long lunge line, and I start by getting her to first walk and then quietly trot around the mounting block. I keep bringing her into me to have a break, and getting her to stand next to the mounting block. This associates the object with something positive (in this case, with having a break after going forward, which isn't her favorite thing). She is calm and focused on me. The short, varied phases are doing her good. I find that Mona tends to be more calm than apprehensive when we are doing something that is unfamiliar to her, so I dare to take the step. I slowly and calmly step onto the mounting block. I have "parked" Mona relatively close to the steps—maybe a foot and a half away. She follows me not just with her ears but with a sidelong glance. I probably seem more threatening to her in this position. I keep my breathing calm and try not to tense up too much. I also use the tried-and-tested method of getting Mona to slightly lower her head—I can easily reach the crest of her mane from here. So that I can make it clear to Mona that she is doing the right thing, I need to change my position for the reward, so I climb back down the two steps of the stool as soon as she lowers her head.

I try it again after a short break. I lead Mona to the mounting block and climb onto it. She reacts even faster now. I hardly need to touch her and she lowers her head. I take this as another sign that she wants to get rid of the pressure that she feels from me and from above. How must it be for a horse that simply has to tolerate things and is not allowed to have a say in whether the next step is okay? I am fairly certain that many problems in horse behavior stem from this initial overload or helplessness.

I stand on the mounting block again and stroke Mona's back and side with my hand. As I do so, I lean over her slightly, and gradually increase the sweeping touch. She listens very attentively behind her. After just a few moments, I praise her with my voice and climb back down from my mounting block. Her acceptance of me touching her back from above was a first important step. I do it again and put a little more weight behind my touch. I proceed with caution, because I don't want her to get a fright when she suddenly notices me on the other side. I praise her while breathing out to keep myself relaxed. Mona stays calm and accepts it. To finish, I give a gentle pulse on the rope to get her to relax and lower her head again while I lean my upper body slightly over her. What a great way to finish this first mounting exercise!

FIRST VISIT FROM THE FARRIER

Today is the big day—we've got our first appointment with the farrier. During the past few days, I have kept to a similar routine before training in the round pen: Mona and I stop at the tying rings for a few minutes; again, I just pull the rope through the ring. I brush her and work on picking up her feet again. She is quite good with the front ones. I can pick them out normally with the hoof pick. Mona found the first touch on the sole of her foot strange, but with soothing words and a little food reward while holding her foot up, she soon came to enjoy it.

I have got a step further with her back feet. I can now pick up the hoof I used to pick up with the lunge line, with my hand instead. I am still very careful, because the moment when Mona lifts her foot off the ground is still critical. She can still give a kick now and then. I pick up her hind feet for just a few seconds and very carefully pick them out.

I go into the round pen with Mona and the farrier. She is still much more relaxed when she has more space around her.

Now, for the first time, someone other than me is going to touch her legs and pick up her feet. I'm not sure how she is going to react. When other strangers approach her, she responds with curiosity, but if they then touch her, she shows her uneasiness with a quick threat.

My farrier and I agree that we only want to try to handle all four feet. We don't put ourselves under any pressure. I'm glad that we can work so well together. He is also interested in this challenge and takes a lot of time with Mona. We aren't working under time constraints or high body tension.

I stand Mona in the middle of the round pen so that we have enough space if she does want to move away. I hold the rope loosely and chat away soothingly.

Thilo, the farrier, talks to her quietly, approaches her shoulder from the side and gently strokes it. Mona looks around, but doesn't threaten him. I don't know how she will react, but I do know that Thilo has enough experience to handle any situation that arises. I know that he will never respond with violence and that he has his emotions under control.

We have both decided that he won't wear gloves. I have often found that horses are very apprehensive about gloves, especially scratchy safety gloves. Even though Thilo is slightly compromising on safety, there is a better chance that Mona won't react with fear.

He strokes his hand down her leg, doesn't hesitate for long and matter-of-factly picks up her front hoof on the command "foot." Mona lifts her front foot and Thilo calmly but quickly begins to scrape out her hoof with the paring knife. She looks around briefly and nips him—tenderly rather than aggressively—on the rear. I deliberately don't react, give her a smack, or yank her head away, because that could cause her to overreact. I talk to her slightly more directly and distract her at her head by scratching her forehead.

Thilo puts her hoof back down after around 30 seconds. We are both very relieved that it went so well. I am amazed by how easily she allowed a stranger to touch her leg.

Trimming the excess hoof isn't actually a problem, although this kind of contact with her hooves involves a new sound and definitely a completely new sensation for Mona. She isn't yet familiar with putting her hoof onto a block for it to be rasped, so Thilo uses his hand rasp to round off her front hooves while holding them. He begins cautiously, but when the vibration starts, it is probably a bit too much for her. She becomes unsettled and pulls her hoof away. Very calmly, Thilo tries again and rasps her hooves with slow movements back and forth, which is less effective but gets her used to this strange sensation. We allow Mona to tolerate it for a few seconds and then stop. We don't want to make this situation too unpleasant for her after she's been so cooperative and shown so much trust. The other front hoof is a success. Trimming it is no problem, and the farrier only uses the rasp for a short time.

THE FIRST MONTH

1	2	3	4	5	6	7
8	9	10	11	12	13	14
15	16	17	18	19	20	21
22	23	24	25	26	27	28
29	30	31				

THE SECOND MONTH

		1	2	3	4
5	6	7	8	9	10	11
12	13	14	15	16	17	18
19	20	21	22	23	24	25
26	27	28	29	30		

THE THIRD MONTH

					1	2
3	4	5	6	7	8	9
10	11	12	13	14	15	16
17	18	19	20	21	22	23
24	25	26	27	28	29	30
31						

Now Thilo goes to her back feet. I know how quick she can be with her back legs and warn him again as a precaution. He strokes her hindquarters slowly, talking to her quietly as he does so. Then he carefully, but firmly picks up her foot. It works!

He deliberately doesn't lift her leg very high to avoid unbalancing her or triggering a defensive reaction. I have so far only picked up her hind legs a few times myself. Thilo works quickly and has trimmed her hooves within a few seconds. He doesn't rasp her hind hooves, because they have worn down short enough. The farrier is very happy with Mona's feet and confirms that her hooves are very hard.

Thilo does exactly the same with the other hind leg. I am grateful for every second of trust that she calmly shows this stranger, and we are both very relieved that the first visit from the farrier has gone so well.

It has never mattered so much to me for a farrier visit to go smoothly. I had experienced some quick reactions from Mona, so it was important to me not to put either her or other people in danger. To calmly give a human their hoof when the human reaches for it is a big thing for wild horses. The strong defensive behavior at the start showed how threatened Mona felt. It makes her composure in this situation and the trust that she shows me and the farrier after just a short time all the more astounding. It's overwhelming!

FIRST SADDLING

Today, I want to put a saddle on for the first time. During recent sessions, I have kept practicing lateral movement toward me in short sequences. This will make mounting easier for both of us later, because I will be able to park Mona at the mounting block.

Mona has now worn the pad and the lungeing roller a few times, including during movement. She has accepted the sensation of something large on her back and of being encircled by something with moderate pressure. Saddling will definitely be something different again: the Western stirrups swinging by her sides, the not inconsiderable weight of the saddle, and the noises the saddle makes when the horse moves forward.

I have everything prepared before I take Mona into the round pen. I have put the saddle in the middle of the circle and placed the pad over it.

Then, I lead Mona in. She obviously notices that there is something new in the middle. As with introducing any new object, I work around it with her, do the familiar groundwork exercises, get her to move away from me and take a few lateral steps toward me. Then, I lunge her around the saddle in the cavesson and let her have a break next to it. She sniffs the leather saddle curiously, but doesn't really know what to make of it.

I start with the pad that she has already had on her back two or three times. We do a small circuit in walk and I get her to stand by the saddle again. Then, I pick up the saddle and carry it around in front of her. As you know, I always do this with new objects because it allows a horse to become familiar with the object from a distance and to see that it doesn't just approach him out of control.

It obviously isn't as easy with the heavy Western saddle, but if she is supposed to carry it then I can manage it for a few minutes. I halt in the middle with Mona. I have the lead rope draped over my left arm. I begin to touch and stroke her side with the saddle. It's useful if you have enough strength to be able to hold the Western saddle with your right arm, and to get the horse to lower his head with your left. The saddle is heavy, and I need to put it down after a short time to catch my breath. This also gives us the break we need in this new situation, to prevent the mare from becoming overwhelmed. I repeat this a few times and begin to hold the saddle slightly higher above Mona. I now make larger movements with the saddle from her withers back. I have hung the offside stirrup over the horn to prevent it from banging against her side when I put the saddle over her back for the first time. I want to prevent Mona from getting a fright and jumping in my direction.

The first attempt: I carefully place the saddle on Mona's back and praise her as I do so. She remains in a relaxed posture with her head low. The mare listens attentively behind her, but she isn't tense, unlike me. What happens if she jumps now and this large object falls onto the ground next to her? I definitely want to avoid that. I continue calmly so as not to seem too cautious and not to convey my apprehension. I move the saddle back and forth slightly. She is familiar with this movement from habituation to the pad. There are some new noises now, like the jingling of the buckles on the saddle, but Mona stays calm and trusts me. I quietly go around to the other side, remove the stirrup from the horn and the girth from its holder. I pass the girth under her belly from the left side and do the same exercises as I did for getting her used to the girth—gently tightening it and loosening it again. Mona lowers her head, because she is already familiar with these repetitive touches.

It is important that the girth is neither too tight nor too loose. The saddle shouldn't slip when the horse moves, but the horse shouldn't feel restricted by it. I slowly tighten the girth, but I don't notice any defensive behavior or increased tension in her. It is now moderately tight so the saddle won't slip should Mona leap away or give a flight or defensive response. I praise her and risk the first steps forward. I walk a few steps with her, ask her to halt, and immediately praise her. Nothing has happened so far. She hasn't overreacted! I walk another five or six steps with her, get her to halt again and take two steps back. I also incorporate some exercises that she is familiar with. I walk a small circle with her and I am relieved because she walks quietly behind me, without shooting forward or bucking. She is clearly showing that she trusts me. I loosen the girth again after a few minutes and take off the saddle. I'm happy that we have taken this big step so calmly and successfully.

THE FIRST MONTH

1	2	3	4	5	6	7
8	9	10	11	12	13	14
15	16	17	18	19	20	21
22	23	24	25	26	27	28
29	30	31				

THE SECOND MONTH

		1	2	3	4
5	6	7	8	9	10	11
12	13	14	15	16	17	18
19	20	21	22	23	24	25
26	27	28	29	30		

THE THIRD MONTH

					1	2
3	4	5	6	7	8	9
10	11	12	13	14	15	16
17	18	19	20	21	22	23
24	25	26	27	28	29	30
31						

The first relaxed steps under saddle. Having a low head carriage helps a horse to be more relaxed about accepting the saddle. A luxurious roll is a positive way to end this big step in training.

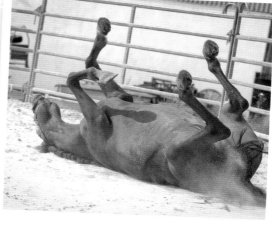

Why Wearing a Saddle Goes Against a Horse's Nature

Probably the greatest danger for a flight animal is to be grabbed by a predator that won't let go. This would cause the flight or fight response to kick in (see p. 8). If you imagine what a loose saddle must mean for a horse when it encircles his body and, in the worst case scenario, can't be shaken off by flight or defense, you can understand how important the right preparation is. A horse that stays visibly relaxed when the girth is done up and he walks forward is proof of good preparatory work.

Mona still watches attentively as I brush her. She is becoming more and more practiced at having her feet picked out.

PRACTICING STANDING TIED

Mona and I are getting into more and more of a routine together. I now groom her in our tying area in the barn more often, where she still behaves differently than she does outside. She can't see around her and she feels restricted. To help her to stay calm, I have to move very deliberately when I approach her, groom her, pick up her feet, or walk around her to turn her around.

Because I don't want to tie up Mona properly yet, I keep repeating the tying exercise by pulling the lunge-line rope through the tying ring. I take a gentle hold of the rope to create light pressure on her poll. When I notice that she intensifies the pressure, I tap her hindquarters gently with the whip to show her that the solution lies in moving forward. As soon as she takes a small step forward, I immediately stop touching her and release the pressure on the rope. This teaches her to look for a solution by going forward, and not to lean into the halter. She should put this into practice later when she is tied up properly.

This exercise is already routine for her. A gentle hold on the rope gets her to take a step forward, and I release the pressure again.

I can now touch and groom Mona all over, and picking out her feet is becoming more and more established. Since I only put the

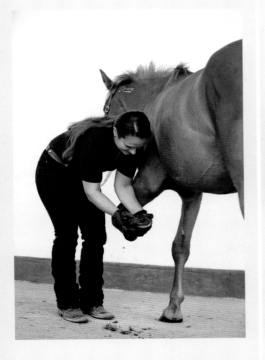

saddle on her for the first time yesterday, I obviously don't do it at the tying ring yet. That would be too dangerous for everybody involved. She is clearly much more relaxed in the round pen than in the grooming area. I get the saddle and the pad ready in the round pen first and then go there with Mona.

I repeat the saddling exercise, following the same calm routine as last time. Mona stands quietly and lets me fiddle about. Today, I want to keep working on the groundwork exercises, but with the saddle. I begin our groundwork exercises right away, leading Mona on the rope. I get her to do exercises that she is familiar with, so the saddle becomes incidental. She focuses calmly on the things she already knows. Then, I get her to first walk then trot around me in a circle on the lunge line, for the first time under saddle. The

sound made by the stirrups and the buckles becomes louder. She listens behind her and speeds up slightly in trot. I let her come back to walk quietly and then trot on again. I don't want her to feel in any way pursued by this "thing." The second time she trots on is much better and I let her go onto an ever-increasing circle. I encourage her to lower her head again so that she notices that the tension on the girth decreases when her trot is relaxed and long-and-low. This actually works well. If I give her a brief impulse on the cavesson with my driving whip hand slightly raised, she lowers her head. I then lower my whip hand again and relax the rope. I want to give her the freedom of the whole round pen for the canter, and take the rope off her. Now she can move a bit more freely. I raise my body tension and give the verbal

The saddle feels different in trot to walk. The swinging stirrups don't unsettle Mona.

THE FIRST MONTH

1 2 3 4 5 6 **7**
8 9 10 11 12 13 **14**
15 16 17 18 19 20 21
22 23 24 25 26 27 **28**
29 30 31

THE SECOND MONTH

         1 2 3 **4**
5 6 7 8 9 10 **11**
12 13 14 15 16 17 **18**
19 20 21 22 23 24 **25**
26 27 28 29 30

THE THIRD MONTH

               1 **2**
3 4 5 6 7 8 **9**
10 11 12 13 14 15 **16**
17 18 19 20 21 22 **23**
24 25 26 27 28 29 **30**
31

command, "Canter," and sure enough, she takes her first canter strides under saddle. The rhythm now causes the stirrups to swing more by her belly. Mona doesn't relax quite as much in canter as she does without a saddle, but there is no wild bucking or resistance. I'm glad that I took so much time.

Typical of Mona, she soon wants to slow down again. I push her on, get her to canter again and she does a few slightly rounder canter strides, but you definitely couldn't call it bucking. They are probably more caused by my own increased body tension than the saddle. Once she has done another lap of the round pen, I let her come back to walk and then invite her into me for a break.

GROUND DRIVING

To prepare for riding, I like to "drive" horses from the ground. It's a kind of long-reining work that gives young horses their first understanding of steering, halting, and going backward, without anybody walking in front of them or sitting on them. You could call it an intermediate stage between groundwork and riding. It is a great way to teach the horse that people can give signals from a different guiding position and to trust them from this position too. To drive

well from the inside. This is also good preparation for later being ridden, because the horse will be used to these movements in the saddle. I lunge Mona like this in both directions until she is walking and trotting around me very calmly.

I then attach both lunge lines to the sidepull function of the cavesson, feed both of them through the large stirrups of the Western saddle and stroke her hindquarters with the lunge lines again diagonally from behind. To familiarize the horse with this guiding position, I get her to walk around me in a small circle again, like I did before, except this time, the outside rein is containing Mona from the outside and also resting gently against her hindquarters. This causes her to speed up, but she neither panics nor charges off. She just doesn't know what to think of this unfamiliar encircling contact yet.

I soothe her and get her to walk again, which also releases the pressure on the outside rein. I get her to walk around me on both reins (similar to lungeing with two lines) before positioning myself behind her. The next thing I want to show her is halting in response to a voice command—which she already knows—and gently taking up the reins. It's especially important to me that I can always get her to halt. She has to get to know the meaning of the reins as a boundary from the ground, before I sit on her for the first time.

To make the meaning of the reins for steering clear to her, I stand close in front of her and give pulses to the side on both sides of the cavesson. I release the reins as soon as she yields in the respective direction. I repeat this several times on both sides. She very quickly learns the right reaction for releasing the pressure: she realizes what a

the horse from the ground, you gradually have to get the horse used to the feeling of the lunge lines touching his sides and hindquarters. Some horses do not react well to being touched by the rope along and down their hind legs.

Mona is already familiar with the lunge line touching her hindquarters from the preparatory work for picking up her feet. Nevertheless, I still proceed with caution. It's essential that she doesn't get a fright or panic when I begin the first exercises with her. I stroke her all over with the lunge line and also prepare her for the stirrups moving when I pull the lunge lines through them. I lunge her with the single lunge line first. The stirrups move farther away from her when I take up the rein. They come into her field of vision, which she finds quite strange at first. By taking up and releasing the lunge line, I can control this movement sideways pull on the reins means and that the solution is to release the pressure. She is familiar with the word "Walk" for going forward to walk from halt. I have my whip in my hand, give the command and tap her gently on her hindquarters to get the first steps in the "driving position." After a few steps, I halt again, then slacken the reins and let them swing gently against her. I release the reins for a moment and let her stand—and, lo and behold, Mona lowers her head. Because this gentle swinging movement has often meant lowering her head, we astonishingly have our first command for relieving tension at a distance—how wonderful!

I let her walk on again and try the first turn. To do this, I tap Mona gently on the outside of her hindquarters and hold the outside rein against her body. I use a slight inside bend to show her the new direction and the first small turn actually works. I immediately get Mona to halt and praise her. I am very surprised that she also accepts me from this position, and can transfer my commands so quickly. Now I try the first steering exercises on both sides. After a successful halt, we finish the exercise. I take off the saddle and bridle and we leave the round pen.

Transferring Knowledge to New Situations

Transferring knowledge to different situations further establishes what has been learned. You can make use of this when transferring to different leading positions.

Driving from the ground or long-reining shows the horse that different leading positions are possible. The horse learns to transfer signals into this new situation and later to being ridden. The driving position diagonally behind the horse is an interim stage between walking in front of the horse (next to the horse's head) and riding (leading position on top of the horse). The horse transfers the signals to this new position, and understands being led and guided from above.

FIRST TIME IN THE INDOOR ARENA

I set off with Mona toward the indoor arena, where she hasn't been before. I wanted her to trust me before getting to know this large, enclosed space. Our indoor arena has an open design. Tarpaulin walls and wind nets make it very light, and you can see outside on all sides. When it's windy, you can hear the straps flapping or,

THE FIRST MONTH

1 2 3 4 5 6 7
8 9 10 11 12 13 14
15 16 17 18 19 20 21
22 23 24 25 26 27 28
29 30 31

THE SECOND MONTH

                1 2 3 4
5 6 7 8 9 10 11
12 13 14 15 16 17 18
19 20 21 22 23 24 25
26 27 28 29 30

THE THIRD MONTH

                    1 2
3 4 5 6 7 8 9
10 11 12 13 14 15 16
17 18 19 20 21 22 23
24 25 26 27 28 29 30
31

The indoor arena is a new place that Mona is getting to know. Because the walls of the arena are open and give a clear view outside, she can also relax in this new environment.

occasionally, the tarpaulins fluttering. All of this has stopped me from showing her the indoor arena yet. The arena has a spacious entrance area with a 15-foot-wide entrance door, so Mona doesn't have to go through a narrow passageway, which is a big advantage. She hesitates the first time I try to take her into the arena. After a brief moment, I am able to convince her to come with me, and we walk onto the soft, sandy floor.

She looks around, but she doesn't appear to feel particularly hemmed in here. This is probably because there are no solid walls and she has a clear view outside. I intentionally don't walk around the track with her to show her everything. Instead, I want her to rely on me and take her lead from my calmness. She is obviously allowed to look around, but I immediately start getting her

to do small exercises so she concentrates on me, which is always what I do with horses in a new environment. I don't want to let them be responsible for deciding whether or not something is dangerous. She is welcome to sniff new objects, but I don't want her attention to be on the new things. I want to bring relaxation and calm into the new situation with familiar exercises.

This is what I do with Mona, too, by getting her to do our familiar groundwork exercises. I keep getting her to halt, take a few steps back, yield her shoulders and hindquarters and stand for a few moments in a relaxed halt.

She accepts it very well, even though I can tell that she is more tense and a little unsettled by these new surroundings. I only work with her for around 10 minutes, before leaving the arena.

TRAILER TRAINING

I believe that every horse should be trained to load with as little stress as possible—including in an emergency—and that's what I want for my Mustang, too.

The first time I saw her being loaded was at the airport in Frankfurt. It did take a few minutes, but it was calm, without any stress or rushing. Preparation for loading was one of the most important foundations that the trainer in the United States worked on intensively. Thanks to her training, it was possible to load Mona into a trailer, and even walking her into a flight container went smoothly.

Without practice and experience, a horse will naturally always associate traveling in a trailer with stress and insecurity.

For training Mona, I have parked my trailer in the middle of the parking lot at our farm. I normally use a loading method where I contain the horse from behind with a whip and then lead from diagonally in front of him.

Mona already knows this "contained forward movement" exercise from groundwork we've done. You are basically in the position you would be for lungeing, just closer to the horse. By containing the horse, you can give him stability in front and behind, but also have a subtle and precise effect.

As soon as the horse stops, you start to gently touch his quarters. As soon as the horse moves forward, you stop the driving aid. Following this principle, you move closer to the trailer, but keep allowing the horse to back away from the trailer, to show him the path away from the scary object.

When Mona spots the trailer, she looks and stands still at first. She occasionally does this when I lead her. It doesn't matter whether we are going toward the round pen or the stall, and it is usually connected with her seeing grass and her way of always clearly showing what does and doesn't suit her.

It's the same in this case—she associates the trailer with effort, and that isn't her first choice. She is familiar with the gentle forward touch that I am now using as we approach the trailer.

Mona isn't anxious. Walking into the trailer just isn't what she had in mind. I keep letting her go backward slightly and then getting her to go forward again. We manage to get her to take a step onto the ramp, and then she goes calmly backward. Unlike many other horses, Mona is perfectly prepared to vehemently resist the pressure that the halter exerts on her poll, for some time. This is her way of showing that she is thinking and deciding for herself whether or not it makes sense for her to do what I want her to do. During the

THE FIRST MONTH

1	2	3	4	5	6	7
8	9	10	11	12	13	14
15	16	17	18	19	20	21
22	23	24	25	26	27	28
29	30	31				

THE SECOND MONTH

			1	2	3	4
5	6	7	8	9	10	11
12	13	14	15	16	17	18
19	20	21	22	23	24	25
26	27	28	29	30		

THE THIRD MONTH

					1	2
3	4	5	6	7	8	9
10	11	12	13	14	15	16
17	18	19	20	21	22	23
24	25	26	27	28	29	30
31						

trailer training, I notice that she no longer just resists the pressure, but intensifies it so that she pulls me back with her, deliberately using her strength.

I am very familiar with these situations from our domesticated horses. However, they often stop exerting the counterpressure within moments, as soon as they notice their decision to move forward immediately makes it more comfortable for them. Even if our domesticated horses have inadvertently learned to work against pressure as a solution, they change to an alternative behavior relatively quickly if it removes the pressure and gives them relief.

This is different than the learned behavior of using pressure to release pressure. Horses that show this behavior will pull their handlers along behind them until he or she lets go. This is usually something that humans have inadvertently taught the animal, because their timing for allowing the horse to find a solution wasn't right in the first place.

I don't want to encourage this learning behavior in Mona, so maintain the pressure even when she pulls back. I use our preliminary exercise with the flag that is familiar to her from our round pen work. I look at her shoulder and get her to take at least a couple of steps toward me using my gaze (I am a few feet away from her) and the whip.

We keep starting again, because this "discussion" is basically a matter of principle. Who can calmly and persistently stick to their plan for the longest? Mona? Or can I? Mona has enormous willpower. She doesn't become wild, but uses her immense strength very deliberately.

I persist and get her back on the ramp again.

I'm going to change my strategy—I am now having to rethink the principle that has so far worked with every single domesticated horse. This horse is obviously always going to decide for herself whether a situation is beneficial to her—or not!

I change course and give her a few alfalfa pellets every time she puts a foot on the ramp. Her motivation changes instantly. It's important to me that I am not luring her. I only want to reinforce her cooperation and increase her motivation to follow my signals.

It works much better now and she comes into the trailer with me. This "matter of principle" again shows me how much natural will to survive and self-determination this horse has.

After the slightly more exciting trailer training, we go into the arena for the second time. I don't want her to be distracted by external stimuli so I have already taken some cones and poles in there. I want to use these objects to get her to focus specifically on an exercise. This exercise should help Mona to associate the arena with something positive. She is familiar with walking between cones (two cones at a distance of around 4 feet) and the poles from the round pen. I guide her between the cones a few times using the command "through," and over the poles with "over." She manages this transfer of knowledge well. She pays attention to me and is very focused on doing everything right. I give her a small food reward when she cooperates well. I now bring a few spooky objects into the arena. First, I stroke her with a plastic bag and she tolerates the touches and sounds more and more.

The pool noodle is new to Mona. I can't make it nice and small like a plastic bag, so I touch her with its full length. She looks skeptically in the direction of the pink noodle, but immediately notices here, too, that I stop bothering her with it as soon as she lowers her head. I can now specifically trigger head-lowering by gently tapping her belly with the noodle. This is a good step for later being able to get her to lower her head when I am riding, by gently swinging my legs. We finish our training session at a moment when we are relaxed. I allow her to graze a little as a reward.

WEEK 4

FIRST WORK AT LIBERTY

I have been working Mona in the round pen without a rope or direct contact. Today, I want to try out this work at liberty in the arena for the first time. There is considerably more space for evasion in here, and it will become clear whether she already has a good bond with me because of our communication work—if she moves away from me, we still have to establish that connection. We start by walking over poles and through cones on the lead rope. I want Mona to focus on me. My praise motivates her, and I have a good feeling when I unclip the rope.

I stick with the exercises and start sending her through the cones at liberty. She gets verbal praise and a food reward after each time she walks through them. I also send her over the pole and she pays close attention to me. However, Mona also tries to find her own solutions and heads straight for the cones or the poles if I don't give her a command and let her decide for herself. It is amazing to see how quick on the uptake she is! I obviously don't want to encourage Mona to anticipate or even to demand food, but her cooperation and high motivation are wonderful to see. Her behavior is in no way pushy and anticipating food doesn't make her stressed. I have seen some horses becoming stressed when they anticipate food and frantically reeling off behaviors in order to get a reward.

Yielding the forehand and hindquarters and lateral movement at liberty are also successful in the arena, and Mona has decided to stay with me during training. It's a great feeling!

I send her through the cones around me in ever-increasing turns until we are doing our first circles of "free lungeing." What this Mustang mare demonstrates after just a few sessions takes a lot of time, patience, and weeks of training in other horses!

THE FIRST MONTH

1	2	3	4	5	6	7
8	9	10	11	12	13	14
15	16	17	18	19	20	21
22	23	24	25	26	27	28
29	30	31				

THE SECOND MONTH

		1	2	3	4
5	6	7	8	9	10	11
12	13	14	15	16	17	18
19	20	21	22	23	24	25
26	27	28	29	30		

THE THIRD MONTH

				1	2
3	4	5	6	7	8	9
10	11	12	13	14	15	16
17	18	19	20	21	22	23
24	25	26	27	28	29	30
31						

Mona is very motivated during liberty work. Sending her through the cones immediately gives her an exercise to do at liberty for which she gets praise.

We also manage to do the yielding exercises right away at liberty in the arena.

Mona follows me at liberty in walk and trot. I contain her with a second whip that I use on the outside.

Mona also stays with me on our first circles at liberty. She understands what I want from her from my body language and the whip.

The mare puts a lot of trust in me and stays relaxed while lying down. For the first time, she really seems to enjoy my touch.

Then it happens—once the work is done, Mona wants to roll in the fine sand of the arena, and I let her. She rolls luxuriantly in the sand, and then stays lying calmly there. I approach her cautiously, but she makes no move to get up. I start to stroke her head and neck and, for the first time, I feel that she is really enjoying it!

This genuine, relaxed, and calm togetherness lasts for minutes. It's an incredible moment.

Horses Lie Down When They Feel Safe

Always being prepared for flight is vitally important for horses. They only show the comfort behavior of rolling and staying relaxed and lying down afterward, when they feel completely safe and secure in a situation. When the situation is relaxed and all the other horses are calm, they can relax and recharge their batteries. When a horse stays relaxed while lying down in your presence, he is saying that he feels safe and that you, or the situation, offer him protection.

FIRST FIGURE EIGHT AT LIBERTY

Today, we are recording a teaching video on the subject of "Learning, Attention, and Communication Between People and Horses." I set up a camera and calmly explain between exercises what I am doing with the Mustang and why it is important for her further training.

We work with poles, cones, and the pool noodles that she is already familiar with. We can already take a few lateral steps along the poles. I use the pole lane to show her that she should go straight when walking backward. The poles are useful for containing the horse and give her a visual boundary to use as a guide. After the initial exercises for encouraging concentration, I send Mona through the cones at liberty. I have set up the cones in a square and I can get Mona to do her first figure eight at liberty through them. This means that I can now get her to do a change of rein from our circles at liberty, just because she has made the link between the exercises!

I bring the familiar steps into a sequence to make it clear to Mona what I want from her.

A VISIT FROM THE OSTEOPATH

Today, Mona is going to have her first treatment from an osteopath (a practitioner who works to improve health, well-being, and performance by maximizing musculoskeletal function and normalizing overall function of the whole body). She accepted the farrier really well, but touching her all over her body is still a challenge. Even when I touch her, she still responds with annoyance or a defensive reaction, especially when my body tension is too high.

Before the treatment, I do some relaxed work with her in the round pen and let the osteopath watch. Mona is relaxed and cooperative, and I work with her on a long line. I then get her to halt at the mounting block and lean over her back slightly—just for a brief moment. Then, I climb down from the stool. This gives the osteopath an initial picture of what we have worked on so far and lets him see her moving. I clear away the equipment and invite the osteopath into the round pen.

I make the conscious decision to have the examination done in her familiar "work area." This was the right decision when she had her feet done for the first time.

This time is different. Perhaps she saw the work with me as too playful and easy. The osteopath walks up to Mona matter-of-factly and, to greet her, places his hand on her back without any pressure. At that moment, she swings her head around and tries to fend him off with a bite. The osteopath—himself a very calm and circumspect person—raises his hand slightly to protect himself, and Mona leaps to the side. Neither of us had expected this overreaction. She clearly still finds being touched by a stranger threatening. We start again, and I ask the therapist to approach her passively.

Mona accepts his touch on the second, very deliberate approach. I keep stroking her head throughout. The osteopath is only going to treat her very cautiously today. He releases a small blockage on one of her front legs with a gentle circling motion. Mona finds this uncomfortable, which she makes clear by snapping in his direction. We leave it at a short basic treatment because I don't want her to associate this new situation with something negative. I also don't want to encourage her apprehension about strangers. To finish, the osteopath strokes her calmly, and the treatment ends on a positive note for Mona.

THE FIRST MONTH

1 2 3 4 5 6 **7**
8 9 10 11 12 13 **14**
15 16 17 18 19 20 **21**
22 23 24 25 26 27 **28**
29 30 31

THE SECOND MONTH

1 2 3 **4**
5 6 7 8 9 10 **11**
12 13 14 15 16 17 **18**
19 20 21 22 23 24 **25**
26 27 28 29 30

THE THIRD MONTH

1 **2**
3 4 5 6 7 8 **9**
10 11 12 13 14 15 **16**
17 18 19 20 21 22 **23**
24 25 26 27 28 29 **30**
31

Associating Situations with Something Positive

The ability to associate situations with positive or negative feelings is crucial for horses' survival. When we put young horses in a new situation, it should at least end on a good note so they can store it as a positive experience. If a horse associates a situation with something negative, he will avoid it in future, which can lead to fear of certain situations, objects, or people.

MOUNTING FOR THE FIRST TIME

We are now able to saddle up in the grooming area. Mona is more relaxed in the round pen, but I also want to establish a routine in our everyday life. I want her to realize that being saddled up in the grooming area is normal, and to relax.

The mare can follow every step during saddling. She puts her ears back out of interest.

1

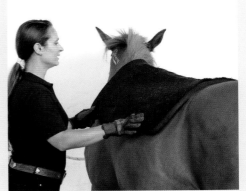
2

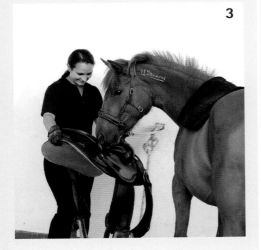
3

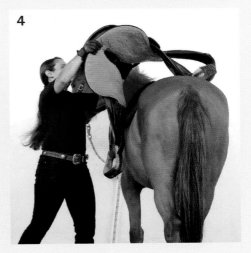
4

5

6

Long-reining is going well now, too, and we are able to steer, halt, and take a few steps back. When I swing the reins, Mona lowers her head and relaxes, even if I am behind her. This makes me feel well-prepared for getting on for the first time. She also calmly accepts me leaning over her from the mounting block. I can get her to lower her head by gently patting her side with my hand. As soon as she cooperates and relaxes, I remove the pressure and climb down. Relaxation is always followed by a reward. If I asked too much of her at this moment or just kept going, I would probably lose her trust.

Mental Overload

Not mentally overloading a young horse prevents him from entering a state of "learned helplessness." You see many riding horses later in life that have not learned to influence a situation themselves. Introducing head-lowering for relaxation and active cooperation enables the horse to influence a situation making him feel that he has a say. This can prevent the horse from feeling mentally overloaded, switching off, and entering a state of "learned helplessness" (in the case of introverted horses) or trying to defend himself against the pressure (extroverted horses).

THE FIRST MONTH

1	2	3	4	5	6	**7**
8	9	10	11	12	13	**14**
15	16	17	18	19	20	**21**
22	23	24	25	26	27	**28**
29	30	31				

THE SECOND MONTH

		1	2	3	**4**
5	6	7	8	9	10	**11**
12	13	14	15	16	17	**18**
19	20	21	22	23	24	**25**
26	27	28	29	30		

THE THIRD MONTH

					1	**2**
3	4	5	6	7	8	**9**
10	11	12	13	14	15	**16**
17	18	19	20	21	22	**23**
24	25	26	27	28	29	**30**
31						

Today, I have reached the point where I want to try getting on Mona for the first time. After our preliminary work, I feel that Mona will stand calmly by the mounting block. I lean my upper body over her back twice then climb back down from the mounting block. When I am back on the mounting block, I swing my leg over the saddle. I keep my upper body leaning slightly forward in the direction of her neck, so I don't sit up too quickly. I have already moved about on the mounting block to show her that I can move above her. She tolerated it without any issues. Nevertheless, doing it in combination with the new weight on her back could cause her to behave differently. I sit up slowly, praise her, and gently swing my legs. I am completely relaxed as I sit on her, and it actually works—Mona lowers her head shortly after being sat on for the first time! The transfer of knowledge that she has already learned has worked perfectly. I dismount again immediately.

FIRST STEPS UNDER SADDLE

Sitting on a horse for the first time and riding away for the first time are two different things for me. The first thing the horse needs to calmly understand is that someone is sitting on him but that nothing is happening. Riding away is a completely different matter. If the object on the horse's back starts to move with him, it could cause him to panic.

I have prepared for the first steps under saddle from the ground by establishing a command for walk: a slight touch with the whip and the command, "Walk." Mona is already familiar with this from her work on long reins and makes the connection. I am, therefore, hoping that she will respond to this signal the first time she is ridden away, take a few steps, and that I can stop her again, which I have also shown her on long reins.

I don't want to get into a situation where the horse gets frightened underneath me and I can't get off. That's why it was so important for me to teach the horse the basics of steering and, particularly, stopping, first. Now we will see whether what she has learned has become so established that Mona can also transfer it to this new situation—with me on her back.

Like the day before, I get on from the mounting block. She is calm and lets me do it. I try to get Mona to lower her head again as she stands. Everything is calm. I hold the whip in one hand, touch her gently from behind and say the word, "Walk." She interprets the first touch with the whip from above different to the way she reacted when it came from the ground, gets a fright, and starts forward. I try to relax again immediately and not to convey any fear. This is a very sensitive moment. If something goes wrong now, she could forever associate it with this situation. My exhalation, combined with a long, drawn-out, "Whoa," and taking the reins, makes her stand, and I can reassure her again. I try to get her to walk on again by gently swinging my legs and giving her a gentle touch with the whip. This time, she takes a few quiet steps and I am able to stop her again. I'm happy that we have done so well! I praise her, dismount, and leave it for today.

The Horse's First Experiences with a Rider

All too often backing young horses is something that just happens to them. One person lunges the horse, another person holds onto him, and a third tries to get onto him as quickly as possible. This doesn't give the horse the chance to listen to stimuli from the humans or to build up trust in them. The horse either takes off or defends himself as a result, and all the person on top can do is stay on. At the same time, they try to keep lungeing the horse. Someone sitting on his back for the first time is a delicate moment for a horse, and this one would definitely develop negative associations with it. A horse may never get over feeling overwhelmed at this moment and be afraid of the person on his back as a result, but not really being able to defend himself. This is not a good start. Backing should be done gradually and be as relaxed as possible. This is the only way the horse can associate it with something positive.

A LITTLE FRIGHT

I have so far practiced mounting and riding away in the round pen, because it gives us both confidence. With the solid boundary fence and the enclosed space, I don't need to worry about being out of control, should Mona take off. I don't want to get into that situation in the first place.

Normally, when I back a horse, we are able to do a few steps more every day. Before the first trot, I start riding a few turns in walk and gradually work toward the faster gaits. Today, Mona had something else in mind other than calmly doing a little walk with me!

When I wanted her to go forward, she immediately shifted up two gears. First she trotted then she went into canter. It was a worrying moment, for me! I have actually never experienced a young horse changing into a faster gait of his own accord after some quiet moments of preparation. After a circuit in canter—with no bucking or defensive behavior—I manage to relax and get Mona to come back to walk by gently taking the reins. We have now got our first canter under our belt, even though it was only supposed to happen later!

I now instill a bit more calm, let her walk on, halt, repeat it again, and then dismount. This is my idea of backing a horse. Even though we have gone a little too far (literally), Mona is now very calm. This shows that the wild horse in her will not just automatically accept being ridden by a human.

THE FIRST MONTH

1	2	3	4	5	6	**7**
8	9	10	11	12	13	**14**
15	16	17	18	19	20	**21**
22	23	24	25	26	27	**28**
29	30	31				

THE SECOND MONTH

		1	2	3	4	
5	6	7	8	9	10	**11**
12	13	14	15	16	17	**18**
19	20	21	22	23	24	**25**
26	27	28	29	30		

THE THIRD MONTH

					1	**2**
3	4	5	6	7	8	**9**
10	11	12	13	14	15	**16**
17	18	19	20	21	22	**23**
24	25	26	27	28	29	**30**
31						

THE SECOND MONTH

WEEK 1

PLANNING OUR FIRST OUTING

We are traveling to "Pullman City," in Harz, Germany, a replica of a town in the American Old West. I have been invited there, with two other Mustang trainers, to do a demonstration with our Mustangs. We have also been given the opportunity to do teaching demonstrations about horse training with our experienced horses. This means that Mona won't have to cope with her first outing alone. My experienced and reliable Criollo gelding, Pablo, is coming, too.

I put Pablo in the trailer first, and Mona is quickly persuaded to walk in beside him. I wonder how she will behave in the new environment. Will she "catch on" as quickly as she does at home? Or is this all too much for her? All of this is going through my head as we are on our way to our first little adventure.

Once we arrive in Harz, we move into our guest stalls. The stabling has the usual dimensions of approximately 10 x 13 feet, but for Mona, this is the smallest space she has ever been in. She is incredibly relaxed, and I show her the arena where the training presentation will take place the following day. This is her first enclosed indoor arena. She pays close attention to me, and we are able do all of our groundwork exercises. Yielding the forehand and hindquarters, lungeing on the long groundwork rope, and

Our first outing together.

We get used to the arena in our own time and without an audience first. Mona accepts everything very calmly.

even lateral movement toward me all work really well. She focuses on me, even though this is a completely new environment for her—it just doesn't seem to bother her.

OUR FIRST APPEARANCE IN FRONT OF AN AUDIENCE

The audience are already in the arena when we trainers take in our three Mustangs. The atmosphere now is different from when we calmly trained in the arena the night before. I immediately see this in Mona. She is very tense to begin with and jumps a few times when she hears the audience clapping. I try to stay as calm and relaxed as possible, and to do things that she is familiar with to give her a feeling of security. Even though the surroundings have changed, there should still be some elements of stability for her: me and the signals for the exercises that she knows. It actually doesn't even take five minutes for the mare to become more relaxed and focused. We demonstrate the yielding exercises and our work with cones and poles. I explain to the audience what is important to me and what experiences we have already gained together.

I only want to demonstrate things that we are confident and comfortable with. It is still too soon to demonstrate them under saddle, and there would be a high risk that something could go wrong. If Mona came to associate this moment with a negative experience, I would have to go back many steps in my training. I might end up destroying the trust that we have built up.

Mona is becoming increasingly relaxed in the strange atmosphere. We are able to show and explain our work on the ground.

The sound of clapping is the only thing she still isn't sure about. It's an energy that she hasn't experienced yet and it unsettles her, but we keep managing to relax again and to focus on each other.

The next day goes a little more smoothly, and I notice that my older gelding is much more nervous during the demonstration than Mona. However, she doesn't really like her stall. She is very tense there, and when I bring her water and muck out, she would really rather not have me in with her at all. The very enclosed space is too restrictive for her and deprives her of any chance to see her surroundings or to flee.

We explore the "Old West" town, and Mona meets a friend.

Mona is becoming increasingly defensive in this environment, but she accepts everything with curiosity. She feels at ease as we walk through the town.

Generalization:
Transferring What Has Been Learned to New Places

The ability to recall something that has previously been learned shows that it has become established. The ability to transfer something that has been learned to a different situation is called "generalization." Horses are able to do this, and you can use it to keep establishing things they have learned.

After the weekend, I feel glad that I took the risk of going on this outing. Everything went well. Small stalls are a challenge for Mona, but her curiosity means she is always willing to explore the world. "Pullman City" was a little dress rehearsal for the Mustang Makeover that we will be going to in just a few weeks.

A young horse should be able to understand and differentiate between a human's signals. Body tension is an important signal in communication between horses, but also between people and horses. A horse is obviously able to feel the rider's body tension. You can very successfully teach young horses that tensing the muscles isn't threatening, but instead a signal to translate this tension into forward movement, for example. The leg can be used in different positions to contain the horse and for steering. The rider can combine her body tension with signals from the leg to tell the horse how much energy to use in an exercise.

STEERING UNDER SADDLE

I think it's very important to master steering and stopping when working with the horse under saddle. I don't want riding to end in a tense or anxious situation. Today, I am sitting on Mona for the third time and the preparatory work on long reins already enables me to ride some small turns. By gently giving and taking on the inside rein, swinging my outside leg and gently touching her shoulder with the whip, which she knows from the ground, we manage our first turn in walk. As a reward, I keep halting from time to time and getting her to lower her head in response to the signal from my loosely swinging legs. It's wonderful to see that she understands what I want from her.

I am currently working with body tension and relaxation in the saddle. I want to get Mona to trot on by increasing my body tension, and to come back to walk by relaxing and breathing out at the same time. Mona can very probably feel my body tension, but getting her to go forward isn't that easy. Only expending energy when it is absolutely necessary is deeply ingrained in her. I have to be all the more precise with my signals and motivate Mona to use more energy.

Because I don't want to tap with my legs or squeeze with my muscles, I always ride young horses with a whip. This is a subtle way of comprehensibly explaining new signals from above, for me and the horse. If she doesn't go forward immediately in response to my increased body tension, I give her a gentle tap on the hindquarters with the whip. As in our groundwork, I release the pressure—that is, body tension—as soon as she does it right. Maintaining the tension would be the wrong thing to do with such a sensitive horse. This would make her either stop going forward altogether or start defending herself. We keep managing to go into trot. I always praise her with my voice the moment she trots on, and relax slightly as I do so. This reinforcement should keep motivating her to put her energy into going forward—even if there obviously isn't any danger to flee. It doesn't take her very long to grasp that the pressure she wishes to avoid even more than wasting energy, releases as soon as she goes into trot. Today, I am very satisfied with our first attempts at steering and our first walk-trot transitions.

PUTTING ON BOOTS FOR THE FIRST TIME

I was expecting something to happen when I put boots on Mona for the first time. She initially reacted very strongly to having her legs touched, so I couldn't imagine that she would just tolerate something

I have had very different experiences with other young horses. They either walk like a stork or want to run away as soon as they see the boots. It's wonderful to have this trust between us.

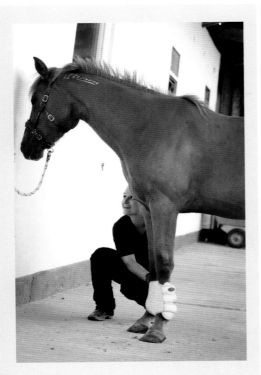

Mona calmly accepts having the boots put on. Given her initial violent reaction to having her legs touched, this is incredible progress.

wrapping around her leg and staying there. I carefully stroke her shoulder, and then her legs down to her pasterns, with the open boots. I act as if I am putting the boots on, but I don't do them up, so I can remove them at the right moment if Mona doesn't allow the contact. To my amazement, she no longer seems to have a problem with something wrapping around her legs. She is in the tying area, but she isn't tied up properly. Because I don't know how she will react, it would be much too dangerous to tie up her front end. After I have put on both of the front boots, I walk a couple of circuits with her. And lo and behold, it actually doesn't seem to bother her!

Why Working in the Round Pen is Easier in the Beginning

If the horse has already learned during groundwork to associate this "work area" with relaxation and praise from the beginning, then it is a good place for showing him new things. When a horse is somewhere he finds pleasant, he will deal with new stimuli and situations better and more quickly and calmly than when the environment itself makes him feel apprehensive. The sturdy fence of the round pen, with its view to the outside, doesn't make him feel hemmed in. If a young horse wants to run away, it will be easier to handle, including under saddle, in this circle than in a large indoor arena. A horse can go straight for longer distances in an arena, and if he is able to pick up speed, could be a danger to himself and his rider. The spacious arena is the next challenge, once the horse has accepted the rider and understood what her signals mean. In my opinion, steering, halting and the basic paces should be established in the horse before riding in the arena for the first time. The educational principle of doing easy things before difficult things also applies here. When you ask too much of a horse at the beginning, you will have to take a lot of steps back. If the horse starts off associating being mounted and ridden with negative experiences, this will stay with him for the whole of his life.

STEERING IN TROT

As I have said, I prefer to get young horses used to riding and steering in walk and trot in the round pen. During the backing phase, horses associate this visually protected area with positive experiences. It is like a "learning circle" where there is always something new to discover, but never any negative connotations. I can help the horse to understand the rider's basic aids here in the round pen.

RIDING IN THE INDOOR AREA FOR THE FIRST TIME

Today will show whether Mona and I can communicate well enough with each other so that she can transfer what she has learned to the arena. Before I get on, I set up a small course. Mona is already familiar with the poles and cones. I set them up on a large circle. First, this means that I can keep her occupied with a familiar exercise and second, I can transfer the circle that we have ridden in the round pen to the indoor arena. I use familiarity to give her security.

Getting on at the mounting block goes well. I haven't positioned it in the corner, but a little farther into the arena. I am able "park" Mona at the wooden stool by leaning back slightly on it.

I get Mona to stand quietly after mounting. Mounting and riding away shouldn't be associated with rushing.

This gesture "draws" her to me sideways and she recognizes it from the lateral ground-work exercise. I hold the whip in my right hand and make circular movements with it. That is now more than enough to intensify the pressure.

I mount up quietly, as I have done in the round pen. I get Mona to stand first, before riding off. I gently swing my legs to get her to lower her head, which is fol-lowed by praise. Then, I ride away: I give the voice command, "Walk," increase my body tension, and Mona translates this all into forward movement. I head straight for the first poles. Shortly before the poles, I give the command, "Through." She already knows the voice aid, but sitting on her is

new. I keep her on a big circle and get her to go through or over the poles. I keep ask-ing Mona to halt. To do so, I sit down, tilt my pelvis, relax my legs slightly and say "Whoa" as I breathe out. I can see that my preparatory work has been a success. She stays focused on me during her first steps under saddle in the indoor arena. I am glad that it has worked so well. She gives me something new every day!

When I am riding a young horse in the indoor arena for the first time, I never go around the outside track. This often over-whelms the horse and his focus drifts away from me. The steering maybe isn't 100 per-cent established, and it could result in a dangerous situation, as I've mentioned.

Why Not Use the Outside Track Right Away?

One of the most important things when first riding a horse is for the horse to be able to concentrate on the person sitting on his back. If you transfer groundwork exercises to the saddle, the horse associates something familiar with something new, and learns the exercise faster. The horse also concentrates on the exercise and on stimuli from the rider. If the horse has learned to yield to pressure from the bridle, downward and to the left and right, before being mounted for the first time, you will find it easier to achieve suppleness on turns when riding the horse for the first time. Young horses find suppleness on a straight line far too difficult to begin with. If I rode a young horse around the outside of the arena straightaway, he would be far too distracted by his surroundings and would physically fall apart on the straights and start drifting around. You can avoid this insecurity by working from the easy to the difficult, and from the familiar to the new, both physically and mentally. The ability to ride straight and to ride around the outside track come with training—and it might even take a few weeks.

The argument that young horses seek support from the edge of the arena is definitely right, because a framework helps them. I give horses the stability and security they need by working in the round pen, and then take on this supportive/stabilizing function as a rider by containing them with the outside aids. This enables young horses to learn how to balance before going on the difficult straights.

Mona enjoys a luxurious roll when the work is done. She trusts me and lets me approach her. She enjoys my touch more and more.

I am very happy with our first successful attempt in the indoor arena. I take off Mona's saddle then do a few exercises with her at liberty, before letting her roll. She really does enjoy it. She always stays lying down and rests for a few minutes afterward.

GETTING USED TO THE ELECTRIC FENCE

Horses need to learn to stay inside an electric fence, both for their own safety, and for the safety of everyone around them. Electric fencing is a challenge for horses that have spent the first years of their life in the wild and have only known boundaries in the form of sturdy panels. I let Mona graze in hand in an area surrounded by an electric fence. I also let her go and walk around me. She has so far been too interested in the grass to bother about the fence. Today, I lead her along the fence on the lead rope.

Inevitably—and this was my ulterior motive—she accidentally touches the fence with her mouth and gets an electric shock. Mona jerks back on the rope. I unclip the rope and let her investigate the small marked-out area in my presence but without me constraining her. She then gets a big fright when she touches the fence again. Instead of drawing back, she runs into the pressure. She doesn't understand why running forward is causing her pain! It all happens very fast, and before I can calmly catch her, she starts running in the direction of the closed exit. She gets another electric shock and runs through the fence. The mare runs straight across the stable yard in the direction of her stall. My first thought is that she will stop next to her stall mate, but she doesn't. She keeps running and goes through the open farm gate. Our farm is surrounded by inviting countryside. Now I need to act fast. I grab her feed bucket with a few pellets and see whether I can follow her quickly, without pushing her on.

I wonder what will happen. She stops galloping, slows, and eats at the next clump of grass, looking back to me, but then thinks that her newfound freedom could maybe be more interesting. She calmly keeps walking ahead of me. Luckily, I manage to convince her that I have something tasty in my bucket. After thinking about it for a moment, she comes to me and I'm able to take hold of her halter. Since our stable yard is not fully fenced, and I am concerned that a similar situation could arise again, I decide to keep grazing her in hand. When she gets new owners, they will need to get her used to electric fencing, preferably in a permanently fenced enclosure with an electric fence running on the inside. I decide to put the issue aside for the moment.

THE FIRST MONTH

1 2 3 4 5 6 7
8 9 10 11 12 13 14
15 16 17 18 19 20 21
22 23 24 25 26 27 28
29 30 31

THE SECOND MONTH

                1 2 3 4
5 6 7 8 9 10 11
12 13 14 15 16 17 18
19 20 21 22 23 24 25
26 27 28 29 30

THE THIRD MONTH

                        1 2
3 4 5 6 7 8 9
10 11 12 13 14 15 16
17 18 19 20 21 22 23
24 25 26 27 28 29 30
31

Why Pressure Creates Counterpressure

A flight animal that feels pressure very close to him—a perceived threat—is no longer able to flee. The only remaining option is to respond to this pressure with counter-pressure or defense. This can also happen during the first encounter with electric fencing. If horses don't learn as foals to pull back from an electric shock, it can result in a forward flight response—*into* the pressure. It, therefore, makes sense to fence in adult horses behind a permanent (wood or vinyl) fence with an electric wire fence running inside it. The solid outer fence will prevent the horse from running into the pressure, and he will be more likely to look for a solution to a shock by pulling back.

WEEK 2

"OPEN DAY"

Tomorrow, we are hosting a public Mustang training event that will be attended by several hundred people. A friend has already traveled here today with her "training trailer." We want to present it, and Mona, in the demonstration tomorrow. I think that this training trailer is a great invention. You can fold down all of its walls individually so you can show the horse how to walk up the ramp and into the trailer, step by step.

This evening, we are trying out the trailer with Mona in the indoor arena. She immediately seems very curious. All four walls are folded down so the trailer is like a big platform. I can persuade her to walk onto this raised platform with me straightaway. She seems to like the view up there. I have Mona on the groundwork rope, and I start to send her up ahead of me more and more. We gradually fold up the walls, and it doesn't seem to bother Mona. I can send her between the walls at liberty, and she cooperates very well with the playful exercises on the trailer. This is our dress rehearsal before our public appearance tomorrow.

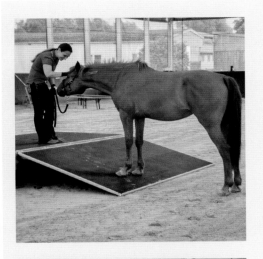

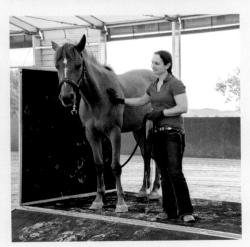

You can find the accompanying video at www.viviangabor.de

We explore the new object. Mona seems to enjoy the new view. She calmly accepts the walls being folded up.

When Familiar Surroundings Change

People are often surprised when a horse is much more nervous at an event at their own barn than when they take him somewhere else. This is because the horse's familiar environment has changed. Horses really notice the difference between what they are used to and a small change. Small changes aren't even noticeable in a strange place where everything is new anyway. Horses often seem to find a completely new situation easier than when something changes about their familiar environment at home. In this situation, you should make the horse feel secure by doing familiar exercises so that he can relax in the new environment.

Today will be interesting. I am excited to see how Mona will accept this changed environment. She has never met so many people all at once. How will she behave? The experience at our first public appearance at "Pullman City" showed that she takes a while to get used to new situations. To begin with, she was really unsettled by the audience with their clapping and noise, especially in the enclosed space.

THE FIRST MONTH

1	2	3	4	5	6	**7**
8	9	10	11	12	13	**14**
15	16	17	18	19	20	**21**
22	23	24	25	26	27	**28**
29	30	31

THE SECOND MONTH

			1	2	3	**4**
5	6	7	8	9	10	11
12	13	14	15	16	17	**18**
19	20	21	22	23	24	**25**
26	27	28	29	30

THE THIRD MONTH

					1	**2**
3	4	5	6	7	8	**9**
10	11	12	13	14	15	**16**
17	18	19	20	21	22	**23**
24	25	26	27	28	29	**30**
31

Mona has never seen so many people at once! She isn't unsettled by the crowd or by her surroundings having completely changed. Her attention stays on me and the exercises.

It's time. We walk into the arena and through several hundred people. Mona seems very relaxed. I talk through the groundwork exercises that I do with Mona. I demonstrate saddling and show how I have taught her to relax. I had already decided a few days ago that I wouldn't be demonstrating anything in the saddle today. I don't want to risk her getting scared. The exercises with the trailer go very well and we can calmly and successfully reproduce what we practiced with it the night before. I am amazed by how relaxed and attentively she focuses on me, despite the atmosphere.

Because of her anxiety about clapping, I ask the audience to start clapping quietly and slowly build it up. After a few seconds, as soon as she stands quietly, I give the signal for the audience to stop clapping. This enables me to incorporate habituation to clapping as a small exercise and to have some control over this unfamiliar stimulus.

What a great day! Mona once again showed me what she is capable of after we've trained together for such a short time. Being this calm and relaxed in front of an audience in a familiar, but completely changed environment is no small feat for a young horse.

LATERAL WORK UNDER SADDLE

From our groundwork, Mona is very familiar with moving sideways in response to my body language and a gentle signal with the whip. Today, we are going to transfer that to our ridden work, which is a new challenge.

Early Lateral Work with Young Horses

I like to start working on a little bit of lateral work when I first start riding a horse. It enables me to prevent the horse from falling into the arena through his shoulder on turns, and to encourage him to gradually stay on the outside track. The horse first learns to cross over his back legs during groundwork, and then to show the same behavior under saddle, just with slightly different aids from above. During groundwork, I use the voice command, "Across." Then, I use it when I give the leg aid and the corresponding rein aid. It doesn't take the horse long to figure out what the new aids (seat, leg, and hand) mean when the rider applies them in the saddle and what the right solution is for relieving the pressure.

THE FIRST MONTH

1	2	3	4	5	6	**7**
8	9	10	11	12	13	**14**
15	16	17	18	19	20	**21**
22	23	24	25	26	27	**28**
29	30	31				

THE SECOND MONTH

			1	2	3	**4**
5	6	7	8	9	10	11
12	13	14	15	16	17	**18**
19	20	21	22	23	24	**25**
26	27	28	29	30		

THE THIRD MONTH

					1	2
3	4	5	6	7	8	**9**
10	11	12	13	14	15	**16**
17	18	19	20	21	22	**23**
24	25	26	27	28	29	**30**
31						

I take Mona into the round pen for the exercise, and ride a circle in walk. I reduce the forward movement using my seat and gently take up the reins, moving my inside leg back slightly to apply the aid. If, at the beginning, she still doesn't know what this aid means, I show her by gently tapping the whip on her barrel next to my inside leg. This causes her to step over to the other side. And there you go, after a few impulses with the inside leg and an explanation in the form of a tap with the whip, she looks for a solution by going sideways. This again shows how quickly horses can transfer something they have learned to a new situation.

I repeat the signal to step across sideways several times within a few minutes to establish the new aid. I let Mona have a short relaxing break at halt in between times. This is her biggest reward. With other horses, it is often a quiet walk or even a long-and-low trot that reinforces the praise with forward relaxation. For Mona, it's still conserving energy in halt, but that might change the more she finds going forward to be enjoyable.

TRAINING IN PUBLIC

Today, some equine science students from the University of Göttingen have come to visit us. They are obviously all very interested in how I am getting on with the Mustang mare and the work I am doing with her. I demonstrate and explain to the

Because of the preliminary groundwork we've done, Mona quickly comes up with the solution of moving sideways under saddle.

I try to focus on Mona, despite explaining what I'm doing to the audience. I demonstrate elements from ground-work on a long, groundwork rope (photo 1) and show how I prepared for girthing (photo 2) and saddling. I demonstrate the head-lowering exercise (photo 3), then I put the saddle on Mona (photo 4). She is now adopting more and more of a relaxed outline in trot—of her own accord (photo 5). I reward this with my voice and by lowering my own body tension.

1

students how I work with the mare on the groundwork rope and at liberty in the round pen. I demonstrate saddling and how I gradually get Mona used to new stimuli. When you are doing a demonstration, you are never fully focused on the horse. In a situation like this, where I am dealing with two things at once, I can get her to do the established groundwork exercises without any problems, but I can't ask her to do anything new. Everyday life is full of situations like this, so I gratefully accept it as practice.

We are able to demonstrate many of the steps that we have already worked on during these first weeks. I am glad that Mona cooperates so well, despite my explanations and resulting wavering concentration. With more experience and security, something that was once impossible to begin with (when distractions made her nervous and edgy) now works well.

2

3

4

5

Tuning Out External Stimuli

In the interests of successful communication, when you ask a horse to focus fully on your signals, you need to do the same. Horses often feel insecure if you are distracted. Completely tuning out external stimuli doesn't mean that you don't pay any attention to what's going on around you. Quite the opposite, because that's the only way you can keep the horse safe. You need to be aware of external stimuli, but communicate to the horse that it is not dangerous and doesn't require your attention. If the horse himself is focused on external stimuli, you should be able to show him that the most important thing for his safety is to pay attention to you. This is how you achieve communication that is built on attentiveness, but also communicates to the horse that you will protect him from external influences or rather, that you will decide whether or not something is dangerous. This doesn't mean working with the horse in a bubble, but creating a safe environment for him where he sees you as a competent leader.

WEEK 3

FIRST CANTER UNDER SADDLE

Today, I want to do my first few strides of canter with Mona. She is familiar with going into canter from our work at liberty and on the lunge line. She goes into canter very precisely in response to the word "Canter" and increased body tension—combined with a kissing sound. Nevertheless, getting her to canter does require a certain amount of body tension and stimulus intensity. She probably wants to conserve energy when moving forward so she can use it in an emergency.

As usual, I get on from the mounting block in the round pen. I repeat exercises like halting and the first lateral movements in walk. In trot, Mona begins to stretch forward and down well and seems to be finding going forward more and more enjoyable. Now it's time. I want to try to get Mona to go into canter from trot for the first time. It's important to me that she can already go into canter from her hindquarters through her back before I try it. I get her to yield slightly to the pressure from the sidepull, just as I have done in walk and trot. This softness on the bridle is the quickest way to get her to do a rounded first canter stride. I don't want her to rush off into canter or use speed to do her first canter stride. The best-case scenario is that she transfers the aids that she knows from groundwork—voice aids and increased body tension—to being ridden.

I prepare her by getting her to focus on me and soften briefly, which allows me to bring a little energy and positive tension into her body. I now bring my outside leg back slightly, give the voice command, and increase my body tension within around two seconds. With a gentle tap with the whip, I manage to get a few strides of canter. I immediately relax, praise her and exhale deeply—Mona is already walking calmly. No bucking and no defensive reactions! I am very relieved. I would prefer her to just do two or three canter strides with a rider on her back for the first time and not develop any negative tension or fear about the gait.

I start again on the same rein after a short break. She realizes that she can again transfer something she has learned previously to the new situation and does some more first strides in canter. I change the direction so we are now going to the right. During our groundwork, she is always showing me that she finds it difficult to maintain a faster gait going this way. I haven't yet found this from the saddle in trot. Maybe it's because she didn't like me to be on her right side when we first started doing ground-work. She has always found work on this side more challenging than on the other.

I do a couple of circles first, which I can also ride in the round pen, and then I go onto a bigger circle. I prepare Mona by getting her attention and by getting her to soften slightly to the bridle, and then I risk the first canter in this direction. I notice that she is tense beneath me but doesn't want or isn't able to relieve the tension by moving forward. I come back into a steady trot and try again. I increase my body tension again and give Mona a gentle tap on her hindquarters with the whip. She goes into canter but does a few very "round" canter strides (little bucks). I try to keep her going forward to get two or three more relaxed canter strides, and then bring her straight back into trot, then walk. She is clearly showing me that forward still doesn't make sense to her. I do the canter transition in this direction again. It's better already. I realize that the idea of going forward is there. I am relieved that we have also managed this step without incident or a violent overre-action from her. I am happy to have got these first canter strides in the round pen without having to do too much steering. I was able to reward her with loose reins as she went forward. It's very important to me that she finds going forward more and more enjoyable and that she doesn't yet feel any pressure from the bridle as she does.

USEFUL EXERCISES UNDER SADDLE

Today, I want to ride in the indoor arena for the second time. Setting up a little course in the arena is a tried and tested approach that gives Mona something to do under sad-dle that she is already familiar with. I put down two poles in the sand approximately 4½ feet apart. I can ride over and through these two poles. Today, I also want to use the poles to transfer lateral movement from groundwork to work under saddle. In her groundwork, Mona is already showing a few lateral steps both in front of and over a pole.

I start on the ground to begin with. I want her to focus on what I am going to ask her to do from the saddle next. I'd like the mare to first show a few lateral steps in each direction, approximately 3 feet in front of the pole; then I'll let her relax and have a short break over the pole. I will keep introducing more variety here and there. I move her hindquarters and fore-hand with my gaze. She should later be able to transfer these movements to rid-den work. I then go to the pole again. I stand Mona directly over the pole and she transfers the lateral movement to walk-ing along the pole. I need to make sure that she doesn't move forward too much but does a sidepass. I stand at an angle in front of her to prevent her from evading over the pole. From the voice command, "Across," she understands very well that this is the same as the movement she did in front of the pole.

These preliminary exercises have made Mona very focused on me. I move the mounting block a little farther into the arena and calmly climb onto it. The mare stands and lowers her head. I am very glad that she has never learned to associate mounting with fear or tension. After a few circuits in walk, I ask her from the saddle to go sideways in front of the pole. The visual barrier of the pole helps her to make sense of this exercise. I wouldn't do the first steps

After we have moved sideways in front of the pole, I try it with her over the pole. This exercise trains the handler's timing and the horse's coordination. If you show a young horse exercises from the ground first, he will later find them easier to do under saddle.

First, I get Mona to stand and relax over the pole. As she is already familiar with the exercise from her groundwork training, I try to get her to take her first sideways steps along the pole.

of lateral work in front of a wall, because I want the horse to respond to containment from the rider, not from the wall.

After a quiet circle in walk, I stand Mona over the pole and she manages to take three steps to one side and, after a break, three steps to the other side. The movement is still a little wobbly and not quite parallel—sometimes her forehand and sometimes her hindquarters aren't square—but that really doesn't matter at this point.

I am also gradually getting her to yield her hindquarters or forehand in the arena, which I have already asked for on a small

scale when working on steering in the round pen. To get her to yield her hindquarters, I bend her slightly to the inside, to make it easier for her to move her hindquarters out. I use my leg slightly farther back and immediately stop giving the aid after two to three steps, and let her have a short break.

Steering in the arena isn't quite as easy as steering in the round pen because we are in a bigger area. By gently tapping her outside shoulder with the whip and swinging my outside leg, I guide her through the poles from the outside and onto a circle on the other rein. I notice that she is not as easy to

Working with various obstacles encourages concentration and precise steering when riding. You can think of different ways to go over or through the poles.

steer from left to right and that she leans against the bridle slightly. I offer moderate resistance with my hand until she halts and takes a step back. I then immediately release the pressure on the noseband. She shouldn't learn that she can exert pressure to move forward or in a certain direction. Even if Mona doesn't have a bit in her mouth, it is still very important to clearly show her the boundaries of the regulating rein aid. Otherwise, this could lead to dangerous situations later.

Working with Obstacles

The aim of training a horse should be to meaningfully explain to him what you want. The horse should see the point of the exercise and be motivated to do it. You can do this by setting up ground obstacles such as lanes and cones in the arena to work on the first steering and lateral exercises. Working with visual markers can also be useful later in training. Working with obstacles not only helps the rider to concentrate better on the line; the movements you use to maneuver through the obstacles also make more sense to the horse with obstacles than without. Riding a lateral movement or even a correctly ridden circle in an empty arena would be a bigger challenge for both. The motto of working from easy to difficult applies here, too.

Mona really enjoys variety and finds it motivating. She touches the ball of her own accord to get a little reward.

TRAINING AT LIBERTY ADDS VARIETY

I play with Mona to keep her work varied. It's amazing how much this motivates her! She has already learned that she gets a small food reward when she touches the ball. Now she will go up to the ball of her own accord and try to kick it away with her leg.

I always incorporate sending her between cones or over a pole at liberty to add variety. This enables me to continually increase Mona's motivation and, therefore, her reactivity to my signals. She gets a very alert and cheeky look on her face when she's done an exercise right and received verbal praise for it—and a food reward now and then. It is great to see her develop her own creativity as a result and start to head for the obstacles herself. This cooperation obviously shouldn't degenerate into anticipation, but I do enjoy seeing her doing it.

Today, I want to try sending her over a pole in trot. I want to see whether we can get her to jump over a small cavalletto.

First, I put the pole between the two blocks on the ground. She is not familiar with them yet, so I want her to just calmly walk through them. When that's going well, I send her over them in trot on the rope first. Then, I take off the rope and do it again at liberty. I am able to bring Mona back to me at liberty after sending her over the pole. She heads for me after the jump if I make the space available to her with my body language. I no longer need the rope for this. Next, I raise my body tension just before the jump and get Mona to go into canter for a few strides (see p. 101).

Working at liberty makes a great change from riding. I can now send her between cones in trot.

First, we practice stepping over the cavalletto on the rope. Mona now understands the command, "Over," and knows what I want from her. We then repeat the whole thing at liberty. She learns incredibly fast and is highly motivated. The mare gets a small food reward when she has done well.

She actually manages a little jump and gets a reward immediately afterward.

I worked on bowing during the first steps with her. When she gives me her leg in response to a gentle tap, I guide her back slightly with the halter so that she shifts her weight back. We have already managed to get her to briefly support herself on the floor and to stay in the bow. She remains very calm, even though she cannot see around her during this exercise.

These exercises are wonderful for getting horses to focus on us as a provider of stimuli and to increase their motivation to respond to us. I like to use them before riding, so after the cavalletto exercise today, I get back in the saddle. I ride Mona in walk and trot, and it feels as if the transitions into the faster pace are becoming more established even after just a few times. The right turn is getting better, too. As soon as I notice the mare leaning on the inside rein after I have gently taken up contact on it, I swing my outside leg and tap her outside shoulder with the whip. This helps her "to think around the bend" and not focus on applying counter-pressure on the rein, and she finds the solution faster. I immediately reduce the pressure when she yields on the right and bring her into a relaxed long-and-low position. She very successfully transfers these short sequences of response and praise from groundwork exercises into exercises under saddle.

1

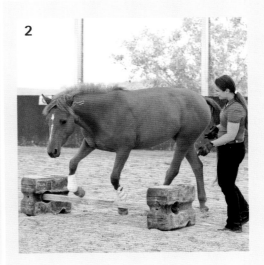

2

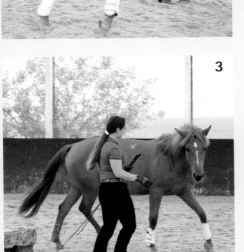

3

4

5

6

101

Mona is scared of the tarpaulin at first, but she is familiar with walking over things from groundwork and is eventually able to transfer this to ridden work. Lowering her head makes her associate the tarpaulin with something positive. She then walks over it fluidly and calmly.

THE FIRST MONTH

1	2	3	4	5	6	**7**
8	9	10	11	12	13	**14**
15	16	17	18	19	20	**21**
22	23	24	25	26	27	**28**
29	30	31				

THE SECOND MONTH

		1	2	3	**4**
5	6	7	8	9	10	**11**
12	13	14	15	16	17	**18**
19	20	21	22	23	24	**25**
26	27	28	29	30		

THE THIRD MONTH

				1	**2**
3	4	5	6	7	8	**9**
10	11	12	13	14	15	**16**
17	18	19	20	21	22	**23**
24	25	26	27	28	29	**30**
31						

WEEK 4

WORKING ON SOFTNESS AND SELF-CARRIAGE UNDER SADDLE

I start showing young horses the first attempts at softness in groundwork training. Slightly taking the rein to the side on the ground should cause the horse to move his head to the side. Doing the head-lowering exercise (pp. 14–15) and simultaneously applying gentle rein pressure during groundwork training shows the young horse the response to rein pressure that you will later want under saddle. A young horse would quickly become overwhelmed if he had to learn from scratch about the rider's weight, as well as steering and softness under saddle. There would be too many stimuli at once. Driving from the ground (long-reining—see p. 60) gives young horses the idea of steering, halting, and yielding to pressure from the reins.

Mona is already familiar with ground-work exercises where she yields to rein pressure. This is obviously not quite as easy under saddle. The new stimulus in the form of carrying a rider, and having to receive and implement signals from this position, is obviously more of a challenge.

During the steering exercises, I can already see that she yields nicely to the side—that is, shows the first signs of bend—and that low-ering her head in response to me swinging my leg and gentle rein pressure is working well. We are already getting a long-and-low outline in walk and trot, which I now want to gradually transfer into self-carriage of the head and neck.

The mare needs to build up the right mus-cles to be able to carry a rider healthily. I transfer a little body tension through my

You can successfully prepare the horse to yield to the inside rein from the ground. When the horse learns how to respond to pressure during groundwork, he will be able to transfer this to the aids under saddle, like Mona is doing here.

legs into the horse and, at the same time, evenly take up the reins. Slight bend on the circle makes it easier for the horse to soften and yield. If I get a brief moment of softness from Mona—that is, a fraction of a second—I immediately give the reins by an inch or two. She needs to associate this new position with something positive (release of pressure) from the beginning. I want her to become more and more motivated to carry herself in this position and to maintain it more and more independently later on. This will develop the right musculature that will enable her to carry a rider.

Mona should carry her nose on the vertical and maintain a little basic self-carriage for a few moments. I use big, sweeping bends for this. She then gets a reward in the form of a break in a long-and-low outline.

Asking her for softness on straight lines would still be too much at the moment. For that reason, I stay on turns, with frequent changes of direction, so the reward is immediately clear to the horse. Changing direction is also a reward, because riding circles one way for a long time is very strenuous. I obviously avoid this, and keep the bends nice and shallow, only riding smaller circles with her when she is warmed up.

FIRST CANTER IN THE ARENA

Like all the other training steps I have established—first from the ground and then in the round pen—I now want to work on the canter in a more difficult environment: the indoor arena. I think that Mona's steering and response to the outside aids are now established enough that I can risk the first canter strides in the saddle. I intentionally do them on the circle because I want to give her the security of doing something familiar and be able to contain her, which will help to balance the canter. If I were to go large right away, she would totally fall apart and maybe even become unsafe. I head toward the enclosed end of the arena in trot to give her a supportive framework, as in the round pen outside. As I raise my body tension slightly for the canter aid and say the word, "Canter," I feel Mona resist slightly. Cantering in the arena is different to cantering in the round pen. I try it again. I need to intensify the pressure slightly to get her really thinking forward. I get three strides, praise her immediately, and let her fall back into trot, and then walk. Her response is almost one of annoyance. Why should she run—in her eyes *flee*—when there is no danger? She doesn't understand why she is being asked to go forward.

Why Run When There Is No Danger?

You might think that running and cantering wouldn't be a big deal to a flight animal. A flight animal has to be economical with his energy so that he is able to flee at any time. It, therefore, doesn't make any sense to choose a faster pace if you don't need to. You obviously don't want your horse to associate riding forward with flight, but you should bear in mind that wasting energy could endanger the life of such a highly adapted flight animal.

If young horses in training often run off in canter, it is probably because of excess energy or because they do not have enough to do and are given too much food and not enough exercise. It's different for the Mustang because she is programed to conserve energy. My timing needs to be good so that the pressure is released as soon as she starts to go forward.

A SCARY MOMENT
A Well-Aimed Kick

It's already late in the evening. After a long day, I go with Mona into the arena to do a bit of groundwork with her. I have her on the rope first and then at liberty. I manage to get her to trot around me nicely without the rope and even to canter a small circle around me. She leaves the circle, but I am able to call her back to me, even from a distance. I have previously worked on that with her on the rope—first "drawing" her toward me by looking at her shoulder (not to be confused with pulling on the rope), then doing it without the rope, and later from a greater distance. By walking backward and intensifying the driving aid with the whip I can actually get Mona to come to me on the ground at higher speed—even in canter.

Today, I try getting her to bow again. I don't have her on the rope. She manages to kneel down onto one foreleg. When she is kneeling and I am crouching next to her on the ground, she suddenly seems to stop enjoying this exercise and snaps at me. As a reflex, I raise my right hand in the direction of her belly and give her a gentle pat with the flat of my hand. It happens very fast: within a fraction of a second she reacts defensively to this "attack" and kicks out with both hind feet! Mona connects with my thigh then jumps to the side. At first, I don't know what's happened and stay crouched on the floor, holding my leg. I have no idea whether something serious has happened—I am too stunned. But then I am able to stand, and there doesn't seem to be anything broken. Mona is standing calmly, with an amiable expression. As far as she is concerned, the moment is over and done with. I quickly realize that I created pressure from my position that could only lead to a defensive reaction. With a slightly battered leg, I try to relax and get Mona to move her hindquarters away from me again. Then, I finish the session on a good note with lots of thoughts about training running through my mind.

Staying Neutral and Fair

It definitely isn't always easy for people to not take personally the things that happen between them and a horse. Even if your horse defends himself by biting or kicking, it doesn't make any sense to take it personally. Every horse person—and especially every trainer—should remain neutral. There is always a reason why horses react the way they do. You should go over the situation in your mind and think carefully about why the incident occurred. This will help you to stay neutral in the next risky situation. If you respond to the incident with anger, no matter how dangerous it was, you end up with a tension in yourself that you can't get rid of at the right moment, which can definitely lead to more dangerous situations. That's why I believe that you should keep working on specifically intensifying relaxation and pressure for brief moments during training to get a stronger reaction from the horse. It's important to switch off this pressure immediately, first, as a reward for the right response, and second, to show the horse that every pressure situation that you cause quickly comes to an end. This is something that should be trained in both horse and handler, because it enables you to deal better with tension and relaxation yourself, and teaches the horse that even a negative situation with you can be resolved in a positive way.

If Mona happens to get away when working at liberty, I can bring her back to me, even from canter. She now has more and more energy that she lets out now and then.

THE THIRD MONTH

WEEK 1

OTHER HORSES IN THE ARENA

Mona and I have mostly had the arena to ourselves so far. I have arranged my training sessions with her so that I have peace—usually in the evening. I know that many young horses pay more attention to other equines in the arena than they do to their handler. Sometimes horses, but also riders, find it difficult to concentrate. On the other hand, there are some horses that find it calming and don't feel "alone."

Today, we have a very quick little Icelandic Horse in the arena with us. Mona isn't familiar with how he moves in the tölt and the flying pace. His rhythm and high speed are new to her. She notices

Concentrating on What Has Been Learned

Science still can't agree on how long horses can concentrate. We know from experience that we have to work on the attention span of young horses that definitely only last for minutes in the beginning of training. It is all the more astounding that my Mustang mare not only demonstrates impressive learning behavior and can quickly make associations but is also able to concentrate on exercises for a relatively long time. It's important to keep taking lots of breaks—sometimes even after only seconds. Constantly regaining the horse's attention, or preferably not losing it in the first place, is a big challenge for us humans. If you notice that you have lost the horse's attention, you should bring him back to you then reward immediately. This prevents strange horses in the arena or any other environmental stimuli that can change in a moment from sliding too much into focus. Being able to recall things that he has learned also gives the horse a feeling of security in these situations.

the other horse but doesn't seem to be that interested in him. I have already found this with her in the round pen. Our herd's pen is just a few feet away from it. There is often a kerfuffle when the horses squabble over the hayrack or the whole herd gets excited. Mona has so far shown little interest in what happens in the pen and has always been very focused on me. For a young horse in a strange environment, I find this astonishing. I can now sense the same ability to concentrate in the arena. Mona's ability to pick things up quickly and to keep her attention on what's important is a key trait that I keep on seeing in this horse. Perhaps it is actually in her nature not to give unimportant things too much attention, so as not to lose sight of what really matters.

CARRYING AN OBJECT
When the Scary Item Comes with You

I want to prepare Mona for many of the things that she could meet in her life with people. For that reason, I also want to teach her that objects that approach her from the side or move above her are nothing to be afraid of. She shouldn't panic if the rider happens to make an awkward movement. Today, I want to practice carrying an object with her. I don't want to pull it behind her, but pick it up, move it over her and put it back down again. I put two barrels in the arena and put a cone on each of them. Mona isn't familiar with the barrels yet, so I obviously let her examine them from the ground. We work around and past the barrels. She hasn't seen cones at this height before. We take a break by the barrels and I pick up a cone and show it to Mona. As I

move the cone up and down at her side, I get her to lower her head and, when she does, I immediately stop moving the cone. This enables her to play a role in this new situation and lets her see that she can influence the movement of the object. Then, I lift a cone over her and ask her to lower her head again. I want to avoid her seeing the cone from above for the first time when I'm sitting on her.

I mount up and keep riding past the barrels in walk and trot. Then, I halt next to one of them, let Mona relax, and carefully reach in the direction of the cone. I notice the horse skeptically eyeing me reaching over. Mona's ears are back and she doesn't know exactly what to make of the situation. I try to stay relaxed and manage to pick up the cone and stroke the mare's shoulder with it from above. I move the cone over to the other side with a slow movement and stroke her shoulder with it again. I keep getting Mona to lower her head and briefly stop touching her when she does so. At an appropriate moment, I put the cone back onto the barrel and calmly ride around the arena a few times. I pick up the cone again and walk a few steps forward with Mona in a slight bend—so she can still see the cone. I come back to halt again after a few steps and praise her.

The moment when the object comes with us is a tricky one, similar to riding the horse for the first time. I am happy that she calmly accepts it. She realizes that the object is coming with us, but she is able to keep walking and doesn't have to run away. After a short circuit in walk, I put the cone on the barrel and feel very glad that she has managed this difficult step so well.

WARINESS OF CONFINED SPACES
Riding Between the Barrels

Some horses find it difficult to walk through a narrow passage. We sometimes find it hard to understand how just walking between two poles could mean confinement to a horse. We know that it isn't dangerous, but even standing between two cones that are close together is enough to worry some young horses. I have gradually decreased the space between the cones for Mona, because I have seen how she doesn't like being lunged between cones that are too close together. Sending her through the cones and then praising her has created positive associations with this narrow space.

Two empty barrels are also useful for practicing going through a narrow passage. I want this to give her more and more confidence and show her that she doesn't have anything to fear from confinement. It will make her feel increasingly sure that what people ask her to do is essentially possible and won't harm her.

She is already familiar with transporting an object from one barrel to another. Now we have two barrels set out in parallel, with an ever-decreasing gap between them. I wouldn't have thought it, but I can see that she doesn't like walking between them even when they are 6 feet meters apart—her whole body becomes tense. She hardly gets between the two objects when she speeds up. I use the familiar command, "Through," here, too. At first, I walk ahead of her, but then I start to lunge Mona between the barrels. At the very end, I send her through them at liberty. She is becoming less apprehensive all the time, but it still isn't a matter of course for her.

I'm glad that I've done this exercise with her. It shows me how carefully Mona protects herself and that she would naturally avoid anything that restricts her. On the other hand, it also shows me that she now trusts me enough to be willing to overcome her inner boundaries. That's often what training young horses is about: losing the natural boundaries that are reinforced by fear and anxiety so that they can get along with us in our world.

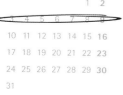

We work on sending her between the barrels at liberty, but she stays on the rope to begin.

Mona prefers the narrow space between two poles to going between objects like the barrels (photo 1). We can also back up through poles placed in an L-shape (photo 2). Well done! Mona gets a break and stays in a relaxed outline (photo 3).

3

Gaining More and More Trust

When training, especially a young horse, it is very important to have situations where initial apprehension turns into a feeling of well-being. You can't influence your environment to the extent that you can prevent a horse from ever being in a frightening situation or being frightened of certain objects. That's what you want to prepare the young horse for. Most important, it can then become firmly established that the horse looks to you for guidance and gets security from you. If you only work in the comfort zone and never go into any situations beyond this comfort zone, then you can't practice what to do when a situation becomes uncomfortable. This can happen, for example, out on a ride when the horse sees something unfamiliar. It is better to practice your actions and train the horse's behavior in advance under controlled circumstances than when such a situation suddenly arises. This increases the likelihood of your remaining calm and assertive in an emergency and of being able to help the horse out of the situation.

The mare shows how much energy she has. Even if we occasionally end up in a tense situation— maybe even intentionally by working outside her comfort zone—it is extremely important to quickly turn this situation into a pleasant one. This helps horse and handler to cope even in precarious situations, and strengthens mutual trust.

WEEK 2

FIRST TRAIL RIDE

Today is a nice day, and I would like to take Mona out for her first ride alone. We have already been for walks together to allow her to get to know the world outside the farm. I definitely don't need to show her the wild, because that is where she spent the first years of her life. However, I want to see whether she trusts me in an environment where she is otherwise used to having to look after herself.

Important Foundations Before Riding Outside

Riders often have the goal, "I just want to go out on the trails with my horse." For a trail ride to be really relaxing and safe, you have to train for it together. Before riding out, the relationship between horse and rider should be firmly established, which means that the horse sees the rider as a reliable leader, as well as a trusted partner that can protect the horse in unpleasant situations. The basics of training—yielding from pressure, relaxing, and being able to accept these signals from the saddle—are the most important prerequisite for being able to calmly and safely explore the countryside with your horse under saddle. When communication works well in a safe area like an indoor or outdoor arena, you can, at least, expect that it will also work well out in the open, despite distractions or unforeseen circumstances.

I AM STILL THE GUIDING FIGURE

We start our first ride outside the arena together with me leading Mona before I get on. As we walk, I want to show her that I can give her security. I get her attention as soon as she becomes slightly distracted, by getting her to back up or take a few steps to the side. I definitely don't want her to stop and stare anywhere or think that she has to protect herself. I notice that she responds much more alertly to her environment out and about than on the farm where she already knows what to make of everything. She is calm, and having to leave the other horses doesn't bother her.

We go into the open country by ourselves for the first time. I walk next to Mona first, before getting on. She is very alert to her surroundings—as a wild horse, she has learned to always be vigilant.

After around 100 yards, I get on and we continue in walk. I now try to give her a couple of exercises and keep asking her to soften so that she walks with a relaxed head and neck carriage as much as possible. She is really "looky," which I hadn't expected at all. When I think about it, I realize, as a horse that grew up in the wild, she will be on the alert in open country. I keep giving her security with exercises that she knows how to do under saddle: we go from side to side of the track with a few lateral steps, and I get her to yield in a slight bend to the side or stretch downward. A short route takes us through the forest, where Mona seems to feel more confident. We have scarcely turned for home but she quickens her pace—even though she doesn't know this route. Natural instinct actually seems to be telling her that she should get back as quickly as possible to the security that she has already found in the familiar surroundings of the farm. The mare stays in walk, albeit a slightly faster walk. Our first ride out wasn't quite relaxed, but it did pass without incident!

Riding Out Alone with a Young Horse

I always start by taking an inexperienced horse out on a trail ride by himself. I keep his attention on me as I want him to look to me for guidance. This gives him security. I could obviously take along an experienced horse who hacks out quietly, but that doesn't teach the young horse to pay attention to somebody that isn't a horse. The rider should also be able to give the horse security. Situations can become increasingly difficult if the horse has initially become used to always having another equine with him. For the first rides, I always choose short routes so the horse doesn't have to concentrate on me for too long. The horse should come more and more out of his natural state of alertness and be able to relax. I gradually increase the duration and distance of training in open country so the horse always feels safe with me.

HABITUATION TO THE BIT

In my opinion, getting horses used to the bit is an important safety aspect. To refine the exercises in later training, you can use the bit to very precisely explain the head and neck carriage and bend that the horse should adopt for a healthy outline. If the rider can be very soft with her hands and the rein pressure, this subtle training work, as well as safety, can also be achieved without a bit. However,

THE FIRST MONTH

1	2	3	4	5	6	7
8	9	10	11	12	13	14
15	16	17	18	19	20	21
22	23	24	25	26	27	28
29	30	31				

THE SECOND MONTH

		1	2	3	4
5	6	7	8	9	10	11
12	13	14	15	16	17	18
19	20	21	22	23	24	25
26	27	28	29	30		

THE THIRD MONTH

					1	2
3	4	5	6	7	8	9
10	11	12	13	14	15	16
17	18	19	20	21	22	23
24	25	26	27	28	29	30
31						

116

unfortunately you too often see horses in bitless bridles that have learned to go into the weight on their nose and become more and more used to pressure. Then, this bridle ceases to be kind to the horse.

I have so far worked with Mona bitless by using a multi-purpose cavesson (Equizaum®). I can use it for cavesson work on the ground and also ride in it using the sidepull function. It also gives me the option of attaching a bit, which is what I am going to try today. Mona needs to learn to get used to a bit, especially for riding out later or for refining flexion and bend.

The first time she has the bit in her mouth, she chews more, obviously trying to cope with this foreign body. I do groundwork with her in the round pen in the cavesson, without clipping the rope onto the bit. She shouldn't focus too much on the bit, but on the exercises that she already knows. I want to make it easier for her to get used to the bit and to hold it quietly in her mouth. When preparing for the demonstration, I consider presenting her in a bit for safety reasons. I will see how she gets used to it in the next few days. Once she is cooperating well and relaxing in a long-and-low trot and in canter, and not showing any excess mouthing, I remove the bit.

WORKING ON THE TURN–ON–THE–HAUNCHES

I start working on controlling the hindquarters and forehand very early on in young horses. Groundwork not only trains the correct response to signals, but also improves the horse's coordination. I incorporate these gymnastic elements and obstacles that are familiar from groundwork into the first exercises under saddle. Control of the shoulders,

Yielding the forehand is useful for steering, for working on the turn-on-the-haunches, and also for loosening the shoulders.

If the horse has already learned turn-on-the-haunches during ground-work, it will be easier to do under saddle.

THE FIRST MONTH

1	2	3	4	5	6	**7**
8	9	10	11	12	13	**14**
15	16	17	18	19	20	**21**
22	23	24	25	26	27	**28**
29	30	31				

THE SECOND MONTH

		1	2	3	**4**
5	6	7	8	9	10	**11**
12	13	14	15	16	17	**18**
19	20	21	22	23	24	**25**
26	27	28	29	30		

THE THIRD MONTH

					1	**2**
3	4	5	6	7	8	**9**
10	11	12	13	14	15	**16**
17	18	19	20	21	22	23
24	25	26	27	28	29	**30**
31						

118

as I have already described, can gradually be used to prepare for a turn-on-the-haunches. If the horse has learned during groundwork how to cross his legs over correctly, so the following leg steps over in front, this coordination can be almost directly transferred to ridden work.

Then, I gradually begin to expand on the turn-on-the-haunches. At this stage of training, the young horse doesn't need to move the inside hind leg in place (as in the Western spin), or to bend in the direction of the turn (as required for a classic turn-on-the-haunches). It is initially about coordinating the forehand, relaxing the shoulders, and getting the young horse to gradually "think" about his hindquarters more. To do this, I practice turns out of the circle with slight inside bend. This teaches Mona the direction in which the increasingly dynamic movement should go. It also helps her to maintain a certain amount of forward movement in the exercise that is increasingly contained on the spot. I also try a second version with her, where she moves her shoulders in rein-back. When you have the horse in a nice backward movement, the hocks start to flex and take the weight, so you can get him to take two or three steps over with the forehand. This is a very nice exercise that strengthens the hindquarters and shifts the weight onto them.

I am still working on activity in the rein-back with Mona. I am delighted when she understands my signals from the saddle and responds to my increased body tension by using her own energy. Now and then, I get her to trot on out of rein-back to train her responsiveness. It's great that I can already work on improving the exercises and putting signals into practice.

We are able to work in the indoor arena without any problems. Mona hardly gets distracted at all. When I sit in the saddle, I feel that there is less tension in her when she responds to my signals than when I work with her on the ground. This could be because of the directness on the ground that she recognizes from being in a herd. Work under saddle is a completely new situation for her that we need to connect with positive associations from the start.

WEEK 3

PREPARING FOR THE MAKEOVER
The Event Draws Nearer

Having gained so much positive experience with Mona, I obviously keep wondering which aspects of our work we should demonstrate at the final portion of the Makeover. I feel very comfortable with her under saddle, and she does her groundwork and work at liberty very well. Nevertheless, I need to make sure that I don't accidentally raise my own body tension too much, especially when working with her at liberty. If I look around at her when we are working at liberty, it is always possible for her to see it as provocation and respond to the pressure with a tense facial expression.

RIDING WITH A FLAG

At the event, I want to show how laidback Mona is. I start working with a flag both on the ground and under saddle. She is already familiar with the flag, because I stroke her with it now and again. I'm planning to fly

We are doing more and more at liberty. Mona responds with incredible sensitivity! However, I have to pay close attention to my own body tension. If it's too high or if I look too directly at the mare, it could cause her to overreact (photo 1). It's important not to bring emotion into it or to correct her strongly. In a situation like this, I relax and continue positively (photo 2).

1

2

the flag as I ride. I can already put the flag over Mona's head and neck on the ground. Today, I want to try working with the flag in the saddle. I put the flag on the wall where I will be able to pick it up. I keep it rolled up to begin with. Once I have picked it up, I stroke Mona's shoulder with it from above. I go into the middle of the circle and start stroking her hindquarters with it and gradually start opening up the flag. I get Mona to lower her head as I do so, and keep the flag still when she cooperates. I manage to swing the flag to the left and right, and to ride a few steps forward with it. This horse's incredible calm never ceases to amaze me!

Canter on the circle is going very well in both directions. Mona canters very calmly for her age and shows nice self-carriage.

Mona is good at circling in canter at liberty then coming back to me. She pays very close attention to my body language and can tell when I intensify it for canter then lower it again as a reward.

PRACTICING SEQUENCES

During my last two weeks with Mona, I want to practice riding exercises in sequence. I start improving our transitions or riding the odd simple lead change in canter. I use the whole of the arena more and more with her, and try to get her to stay soft when trotting in a straight line. However, I can see that she still finds this difficult. If I incorporate a circle, I can manage at times to get her to be soft in my hand, and to show a few seconds of self-carriage.

I also want to practice sequences of certain elements with her in our groundwork. My aim is to be able to show how subtly Mona responds to my body language, within just a few minutes at the Makeover. She is already very good at following me and doing lateral work at liberty, and at yielding her forehand and hindquarters.

I'm wondering how I can link these elements together and what music could go with it for our Freestyle performance at the Makeover. I feel emotional when I imagine our time together being over. I have never felt like this about any of the many other horses I have trained. Mona is special and shows me every day how much we horse people still have to learn from these animals!

EXERCISES FOR THE FREESTYLE

During the past few days, I have continued to work on improving the turn-on-the-haunches with Mona. We have taken our lateral work and are using it to increase and decrease a square for the Freestyle. This week we even managed a simple lead change in both directions! Mona's specialty is a lovely long-and-low rising trot, which

THE FIRST MONTH

1	2	3	4	5	6	7
8	9	10	11	12	13	14
15	16	17	18	19	20	21
22	23	24	25	26	27	28
29	30	31				

THE SECOND MONTH

		1	2	3	4
5	6	7	8	9	10	11
12	13	14	15	16	17	18
19	20	21	22	23	24	25
26	27	28	29	30		

THE THIRD MONTH

				1	2
3	4	5	6	7	8	9
10	11	12	13	14	15	16
17	18	19	20	21	22	23
24	25	26	27	28	29	30
31						

Maintaining Your Own Concentration

When you appear in public as a trainer and have your work assessed by other people and judged by critical eyes, it is important to keep concentrating on what's essential. Important rules are: clear and fair communication with the horse, and not asking too much of yourself or the horse but only asking for what's achievable. Keeping your focus also means sticking to breaks, even when you realize that your time together is running out. Concentration also means staying calm and not succumbing to rushing or pressure. You should be satisfied with what you and your horse have achieved together so far.

Something very special has developed between Mona and me. We are bonded by honest respect for each other and a deep trust.

I definitely want to show in the "dressage" Freestyle. Because I have made sure that she has a relaxed head and neck carriage from the beginning, this has become one of her favorite exercises. It would be great if we could both manage to reliably demonstrate these sequences in this very special atmosphere.

NOT PUTTING YOURSELF UNDER PRESSURE

It often isn't possible to protect ourselves against pressure. And it often isn't even the people around us who put us under pressure, but our expectations on ourselves to do well. I think it is particularly important to stand by what you do. You should only do things with horses that you can morally defend and that you are sure are right. I also think it's important to acknowledge that you and the animal make mistakes. On the whole, you

Enjoying happy moments with Mona and not putting myself under pressure are the most important things for me.

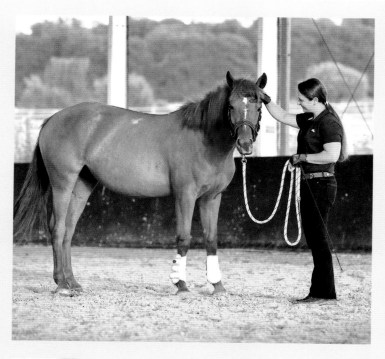

shouldn't put too much emphasis on mistakes. The good thing about the Makeover is that we are able to show what we have achieved so far, without things we haven't managed yet being seen as negative or bad. I think that assessing fairness to the horse—that is, "horsemanship"—is one of the most important points at an event like this.

PRESSURE CREATES
Counterpressure Working on "Throughness" Under Saddle

People and horses respond to internal and external pressure. Both can trigger a defensive reaction in horses. This is still clear in Mona. Here's an example: when she is unsure about or doesn't understand a situation, she still responds to an aid from my leg or hand with counter-pressure.

This behavior causes problems in interactions between horses and people. When a horse works against our pressure, it puts the human in a weaker position and can consequently create a dangerous situation. Just picture a scenario where the horse has to stop at a road, but pulls forward against the reins!

For this reason, it is important to me to show the horse an alternative solution in training situations where this behavior arises. In the few sessions I still have left with Mona, I want to keep working on subtle and clear communication between us. For my part, this means really making sure that Mona is focused on the job at hand—that is, she is ready to respond attentively to my signals. It is also important I work with stimuli at the right intensity and can precisely intensify and release the pressure at the right moment when she shows the correct response.

Communication under saddle is already good between us. Mona goes forward when I increase my body tension, and yields her shoulders, hindquarters, or goes sideways in response to the different positions of my leg. If I use my leg and hand together, I either get a nice softness in a long-and-low outline, or a few seconds of self-carriage on a loose rein.

I keep riding transitions with her but get her to do a lot of work on the straight to see whether we can achieve an outline and softness in a straight line. It gets better all the time. I shift our canter circle from the bottom to the top of the arena or do the circle in the middle of the arena. If we are able to canter a circle in the middle of the arena, it shows me that I am able to successfully contain the horse with the outside aids. I am always astounded by Mona's steady and

I keep training Mona's canter with work in the cavesson. I want to have phases of positive tension where she learns to carry herself (photo 1) and loosening phases in a long-and-low trot (photo 2).

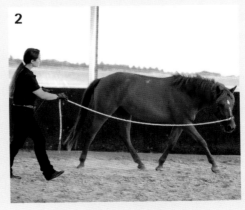

calm canter, especially given her age and the short amount of training she has had. It could be because she naturally wouldn't choose to go fast. Because of her conformation and ability to learn quickly, she can manage to canter at a very steady pace.

TRAINING THE HORSE TO RESPOND TO SUBTLE AIDS

The horse's ability to respond to subtle aids, either on the ground or under saddle, depends on the feel and timing of the human as the provider of the stimuli. Intensifying a signal at the right moment until it gets a response and then being able to immediately switch off the resulting pressure requires the ability to control our actions. Young horses learn incredibly quickly. They can also learn other ways of evading pressure—for example, by going against it (that is, resisting the pressure, or even exerting counter-pressure).

Pressure can trigger defense, which, under natural conditions, sometimes seems to be the most logical and effective response. I have experienced this many times with the Mustang mare. Defense doesn't allow the horse to understand the actual objective of our aids—the horse is rewarded as soon as he yields to pressure. It isn't easy for people to respond precisely in just a few seconds, but it is something we have to do if the horse is going to learn responsive "throughness."

CONTROLLING YOUR OWN BODY LANGUAGE

It is not just the Mustang mare that responds very sensitively to body tension and external pressure. Each of our horses is naturally highly sensitive to body language signals. If horses stop responding to body language signals—as is sometimes the case in our domesticated horses—they appear to have "switched off" from the overstimulation that they experience in many cases. In this case, the signals no longer have any relevance. Then we have the "lazy" horse who lethargically crawls along in his own world, which is often confused with "quietness" or being "laid-back."

In over-sensitive horses, on the other hand, ambiguous signals can result in a horse that has not been able to learn that not every signal from a person constitutes a flight stimulus.

The learning effects behind the signals are very subtle. People sometimes give them without even realizing, and horses pick up on them. Lots of formative learning content comes up in the initial encounters between a young horse and people, and during the training process. The horse remembers how he deals with our signals, to protect or help himself. This crucial initial phase requires

THE FIRST MONTH

1 2 3 4 5 6 7
8 9 10 11 12 13 14
15 16 17 18 19 20 21
22 23 24 25 26 27 28
29 30 31

THE SECOND MONTH

1 2 3 4
5 6 7 8 9 10 11
12 13 14 15 16 17 18
19 20 21 22 23 24 25
26 27 28 29 30

THE THIRD MONTH

1 2
3 4 5 6 7 8 9
10 11 12 13 14 15 16
17 18 19 20 21 22 23
24 25 26 27 28 29 30
31

1

Things can't go smoothly all the time! Making training positive is enormously important, even if the horse doesn't understand new phases of learning (photo 1). You should keep explaining the exercise calmly and clearly until the horse shows the right response (photo 2). Calm and relaxation must return after a few minutes at the latest (photo 3).

a human to have his or her body language and actions under control. The human needs to approach this encounter with control and sensitivity, and to know what actions can trigger.

2

WEEK 4

NEW RIDDEN EXPERIENCES

During the time we have left together, I'd like to add some more experiences to Mona's everyday life. Today, I involve her in my lesson. I sit on her and relax as I teach. She mostly enjoys a break, but now and then I use her to demonstrate how I work on softness or give the aids for the first lateral movements. She does her job well, standing calmly as the other horses work around her. I can always get reactions from her. Mona already has a certain amount of experience, so I can sit on her and feel at ease, and I can now actually concentrate on something else, and she doesn't get unsettled at all.

3

Mona is very familiar with the routines for getting ready in the grooming area, groundwork, and riding. They give her security and don't seem to unsettle her anymore. I obviously try to incorporate variety and more new things into our training to keep her attention. This will definitely also be very important for her future. On the one hand, the trainer needs to provide the security that a young horse gets from consistent routines, but on the other, the trainer also must continue to improve the horse's ability to learn and concentrate. New experiences are important, especially for a horse that is quick on the uptake and so able to learn. They will also prevent a horse from picking up unwanted behaviors.

FIRST UNFAMILIAR RIDER

So far I have been the only person to ride Mona. Today, I have asked an experienced student whether she would like to get on and do a few times around the arena with Mona. I have already worked her today, and she cooperated very well. I've got a good feeling—otherwise, I wouldn't ask the student. I really want to see how Mona responds to a strange rider before she gets a new owner. I want to be able to give a realistic assessment if prospective new owners approach me at the Makeover. We will now see whether she accepts signals from others in the way she does from me.

Mona seems a little unsettled when the student gets on. She looks around and tries to nip. She still shows this defensive behavior in situations that cause her to feel tense or insecure. As soon as she sits in

The farrier visits again to check and work on Mona's hooves. Mona stands as if she has been doing it all her life. She is getting more and more experience in everyday situations.

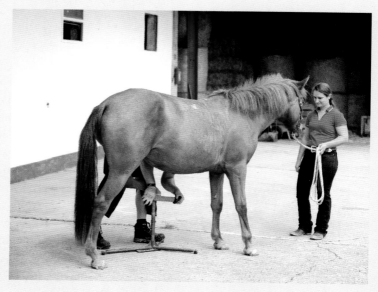

the saddle, the student is supposed to relax and get the horse to calmly lower her head by swinging her legs. Mona knows this routine. It is supposed to give her security and show that defensive behavior isn't a solution in every situation.

We manage a few times around in walk and trot. You can tell that the next owner's job will be to keep working on getting the mare to go forward. It is possible to release the slight counter tension in response to the forward leg aid within a few seconds by just precisely intensifying the signal and immediately removing it when Mona goes forward. She becomes more relaxed with every lap. Even the rider, who responded rather hesitantly out of initial caution, is now becoming clearer with her signals. Mona's trot becomes more active and she stretches down. I am incredibly happy that she has passed this first "strange rider test." All I wanted was to see that the correct responses can be obtained by another rider. At this early stage, I don't want to "annoy" or overwhelm her with more strangers in the tack.

WALK, TROT AND CANTER IN AN OPEN SPACE
How Good Are Our Brakes?

Today, we have a photoshoot. Our time together really is coming to an end. I know that I will soon have to ride Mona in a large stadium, where we won't have the boundaries that we have in our indoor arena. The many spectators and the atmosphere will provide all new stimuli.

I have decided to ride Mona in a few different open fields. We will now see how much she "stays with me" and whether we can transfer what she has learned in the round pen and the arena to a space outside. I basically feel very at ease on Mona. I have never felt that she is excessively tense underneath me or that she wants to get rid of me. However, she still leans against the leg or rein now and then, and tests whether the pressure disappears if she exerts pressure against it. Equally, there are moments when I feel that we are in complete harmony. It's a feeling of responsiveness, "throughness," and motivation!

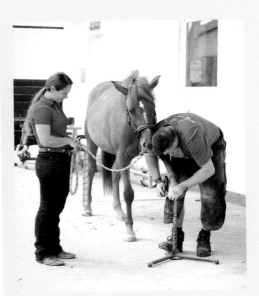

The Mustang mare has to let off a bit of steam before we ride outside the arena today!

130

I'm excited to see how the work will go without any kind of boundary. Out in the grass field, I start working with Mona from the ground. Mona visibly finds it difficult not to snatch at the grass. To make matters worse, there are a lot of flies that I can see are annoying her. I continue with the training nevertheless. I use yielding exercises to work on attentiveness and "throughness."

Mona seems tense and is visibly more "charged" than normal. I let her get rid of her energy by going forward and then go back to quieter phases of groundwork. Then, I get on. This is a very special moment. I breathe and start riding some larger circles with her. It works!

She's great, even in this open space. It's such a good feeling that she is letting me control and guide her so well! We move to a neighboring field. We trot and canter some big circles. The feeling of freedom, safety, and harmony that I experience at this moment is indescribable!

It shows me that the preparation has been successful and Mona really trusts me. She even accepts the aids better in this big, open space than she does in the arena. She obviously loses the circle line on the outside in canter sometimes, which is absolutely forgivable in a young horse at this stage of training. The good thing about being outside is that I have more time to contain her before the next turn comes. She now also seems to be enjoying going forward.

As an animal who loves freedom, she can see much more of her surroundings outside. She seems to feel more at ease without walls and a roof—where she can see farther and move freely.

Unlike when we went for a trail ride and she was watching what was going on around her, we can now focus more on working together. She no longer feels that she has to look out for herself but concentrates on me. She feels noticeably more at ease. I am sure that she will soon also show this behavior when riding outside the arena. People give her security and she can relax in our company.

Experiencing freedom together is an indescribable feeling! You can tell that the mare feels very happy in an open space.

KEEPING CALM BEFORE THE MAKEOVER

It isn't long before we set off for Aachen, Germany, where the Mustang Makeover will take place. During the past few days, I have kept going over our little performance routine, on the ground and under saddle. I ride with a flag, and we do yielding and following groundwork exercises at liberty. I try to fit the exercises precisely with the music, because we only have a few minutes' time for each.

I will be demonstrating a "dressage freestyle" with her that involves walk, trot, and canter. I will also present a little lateral work and a turn-on-the-haunches. These things are going really well in our daily routine, but doing it all precisely to music is obviously a different challenge. I am understandably getting more excited. What will it be like? The atmosphere will be completely different from her previous public demonstrations. How will Mona behave? So many people will be watching. But that isn't what's making me nervous. All that matters to me is to see whether what I have done so far is enough. Has my training method been good enough to stand up under these conditions? Will Mona trust me? What about when the Mustangs see each other again? Will it even be possible to get the horses to concentrate?

These are the things that bother me—not having to do something in front of an audience. That is something I already know about. But what will happen between Mona and me at this event?

HOW MUCH CAN I ASK OF HER?

For our Freestyle, I have chosen exercises that we can do well in our everyday work together. I only have a rough idea of the requirements of the tests at the Makeover. I know that there will be different stages of competition that we can choose at the time. I'm not going to put us under pressure because other people might be further along or because it would look better if

It's pamper time. Mona enjoys a cold shower on this hot day. I want us both to be able to relax. I train her in short and focused sessions with plenty of relaxing breaks in between. We have already come so far that we need to enjoy our last moments together!

Mona could do more. I will decide everything at the time, because I will know what Mona is and isn't ready to show.

SHOULD I RIDE WITH OR WITHOUT A BIT?

Mona has had the bit in her mouth a few times, and we have also ridden with it, but I realize that she still isn't accustomed to the pressure in her mouth. Her response during some yielding exercises is a little more precise with the bit, but she quickly becomes defensive when the pressure gets too much for her. I don't know yet what I will do in Aachen. I'll take the bit with me. Knowing that I have the option of riding her in it might give me confidence. I'll make the decision when we're there.

THE FIRST MONTH

1	2	3	4	5	6	**7**
8	9	10	11	12	13	**14**
15	16	17	18	19	20	**21**
22	23	24	25	26	27	**28**
29	30	31				

THE SECOND MONTH

		1	2	3	**4**
5	6	7	8	9	10	**11**
12	13	14	15	16	17	**18**
19	20	21	22	23	24	**25**
26	27	28	29	30		

THE THIRD MONTH

					1	**2**
3	4	5	6	7	8	**9**
10	11	12	13	14	15	**16**
17	18	19	20	21	22	**23**
24	25	26	27	28	29	**30**

Wir brauchen Gefühl und Wissen, um pferdegerecht zu kommunizieren.

We have arrived in Aachen, Germany. Should I be worried that we've been assigned stall number 13?

THE MAKEOVER
Pure Emotion

We arrive in Aachen one day before the event is to begin. Loading and traveling went well. When we finally get there, there is a lovely reunion of all the Mustangs and the other trainers. It's good to meet them all and finally be able to share experiences in person. It's fascinating to hear how the others have got on. The horses' reunion is surprisingly unspectacular. They accept the situation calmly, staying very focused on their trainers and not even neighing to each other. We move into our stall (a normal-sized stall with a window), and I immediately think it will be a challenge for Mona to spend a few nights in a stall that is smaller than she is used to.

After giving her some time to settle in, I take Mona out of the stall and show her the big stadium. It's amazing how calmly she accepts everything!

I do a few quiet turns around the stadium with her in hand first, and then I get her to do some familiar groundwork exercises. She cooperates very well and the other Mustangs in the ring don't seem to distract her at all.

I decide to put on her saddle and ride her today. Some of the other trainers are working on the ground; others are riding. All of the horses are astonishingly calm and focused on their trainers. Even riding in the large stadium goes well. You need to have the horse well-contained in such a big space, but I can get walk, trot, and canter, as well as lateral work and the turn-on-the-haunches. I am pleasantly surprised, because I couldn't really imagine how Mona would react, especially with the other horses that she knows.

137

The evening before the big event. I can get Mona to do all of the exercises calmly—on the ground and under saddle. What a feeling it is to ride in this huge stadium.

I start by riding with the bit, but then I change. I notice that she no longer feels as comfortable with the bit in her mouth and becomes slightly tense. She hasn't worn a bit all that often. I feel happier with her without the bit and decide to do the various tests bitless.

I dismount after a few successful exercises, show her the other outdoor arena then take her back to her stall.

I put all our tack and equipment in a specially prepared stall next to Mona and make myself at home. I am glad I have my good friend Joanna here to help me and, above all, give me moral support. The time that is now behind me has been intense and strenuous. Now Mona and I need to gather our strength, keep calm, and stay true to ourselves.

We have a few more preliminary meetings today. We discuss the welcome and introduction of the trainers to the audience, as well as the sequence of the tests. We are also handed a list of the exercises we are to complete for the first time. The exercises are easy but will obviously be a challenge under these conditions. Now it's a question of whether the mare will stay with me tomorrow and be able to concentrate in front of an audience.

MUSTANG MAKEOVER
by American Mustang Germany

It's Showtime

It's showtime!

A TEST FOR US BOTH

The tests are underway. We prepare in a warm-up arena indoors. I try to concentrate on myself and on Mona. There are so many people here. The stadium is sold out. Now it's important to stay focused and do what I have planned: ask for what's possible, but otherwise turn it down a gear. I will get Mona to do what she is willing to do at that moment.

We ride into the big stadium: 6,000 people! That exceeds any demonstration or championships I have ever experienced in the whole of my equestrian career. Mona and I focus on the trail exercises. I can feel more tension in her than I did yesterday evening, but we are familiar with this situation. If I keep getting her to focus on me and the exercises at hand, it will get better. She even manages to cross the bridge with me, although she'd eyed it skeptically the night before.

The trail test goes well. We don't do all of the exercises, because we need to take more time for the ones we do complete. I give us plenty of time. Mona walks past a fountain with me, I get on, we back through poles in an L-shape, and walk through two barrels standing close together. Picking up a jacket and carrying it proves too much for the mare, so instead I ride quietly to the end.

Mona's attention is on me, but I realize that it would obviously be possible to do more at home. I'm aware that I am making concessions, and I don't resent her for it at all. I am actually able to tune out the audience, but I can feel the tension below me very clearly. We just do the best we can in the tests, and I try to give her security in spite of everything.

Mona hasn't seen balloons before, but our preparatory work with the barrels pays off (photo 1). Mona skeptically eyes the jacket we are supposed to carry (photo 2). I realize that picking up the jacket will be too much at the moment. After she has sniffed the jacket, I let her continue calmly.

THE FIRST MONTH

1	2	3	4	5	6	**7**
8	9	10	11	12	13	**14**
15	16	17	18	19	20	**21**
22	23	24	25	26	27	**28**
29	30	31				

THE SECOND MONTH

		1	2	3	**4**
5	6	7	8	9	10	**11**
12	13	14	15	16	17	**18**
19	20	21	22	23	24	**25**
26	27	28	29	30		

THE THIRD MONTH

				1	**2**
3	4	5	6	7	8	**9**
10	11	12	13	14	15	**16**
17	18	19	20	21	22	**23**
24	25	26	27	28	29	**30**

The backdrop is incredible. Despite the many people, we still manage to concentrate on each other (photo 1). We are able to successfully show lateral work (photo 2) and the turn-on-the-haunches (photo 3). Mona does her thing in canter, too (photo 4)!

Head-lowering enables me to get Mona to relax even in this atmosphere, and I can get off her calmly. Some of the applause from the spectators unsettles her.

Today, we have the horsemanship exercise ahead of us, a little "dressage test." Walk and trot and a few sideways steps in front of a pole go well. Mona keeps drifting toward the exit in canter. She now knows exactly where we came in and the way out of the stadium back to the other horses. Nevertheless, we manage to canter in both directions, and I am very happy with our performance.

Next we present our "dressage freestyle." We can ride a test we have put together ourselves. We have prepared lateral work, walk, trot, a stretch of long-and-low trot, and canter. The mare does really well. She is with me and I have a good feeling. And lo and behold, our score is actually in the top five! What a success.

Now all that remains is the Freestyle finale. Everybody has prepared a short routine of a few minutes' duration. I am dressed as "James Bond" and riding in to the theme of *Goldeneye*. The plan is that I will get changed on Mona and turn into a "Bond Girl."

I ride in with a large golden flag that I swing around the horse, but I realize that steering is tricky with just one hand on the reins.

To change my jacket, hat, and trousers on the horse I get Mona to lower her head—then I just fling the clothes away. The mare knows this exercise well and manages it beautifully.

Then, we demonstrate a few exercises on the ground to some very peaceful music. We practiced all of it at liberty at home, but when I am in the arena, I decide against letting Mona off the groundwork rope. I think it's too much of a risk. I am moved that it has all gone so well. The atmosphere during the show is so emotionally charged, it's just about crackling. I leave the finale with Mona with tears of happiness in my eyes. I know that the end of our time together is so close I could touch it, and I am overwhelmed by how well she managed her appearance with me.

Big emotions at the finale: after I ride in as "James Bond," Mona stays very calm during my "transformation" to a "Bond Girl" and the flying clothes.

THE FIRST MONTH

1	2	3	4	5	6	**7**
8	9	10	11	12	13	**14**
15	16	17	18	19	20	**21**
22	23	24	25	26	27	**28**
29	30	31				

THE SECOND MONTH

			1	2	3	**4**
5	6	7	8	9	10	**11**
12	13	14	15	16	17	**18**
19	20	21	22	23	24	**25**
26	27	28	29	30		

THE THIRD MONTH

					1	2
3	4	5	6	7	8	**9**
10	11	12	13	14	15	**16**
17	18	19	20	21	22	**23**
24	25	26	27	28	29	**30**

I get Mona to yield (photo 1) and follow me from the ground, but I don't let her off the rope. We bow in front of 6,000 spectators (photo 2), and I thank Mona for trusting me in this setting (photo 3).

After the presentation ceremony (photo 1), the auction begins (photos 2 and 3). I have mixed feelings, and I wonder what will happen to Mona next. Then, suddenly...Mona has new owners! They are totally overwhelmed (photo 4).

The last event on the program is the auction of the Mustangs. Now they get their new owners. Two women have bought Mona. Two sisters, as it turns out. It seems the purchase was quite spontaneous, as both women are completely overwhelmed. I feel churned up inside and wonder what will happen with Mona next. Will the new owners get on well with her and Mona with them?

We exchange information and agree to discuss everything in peace once we are back at the farm. Mona's new home won't be far away from me. I will take Mona away with me and will bring her together with her new owners, step by step.

SAYING GOODBYE

Mona stays with us for some time after the Makeover. I train her further and work with her new owners until they all feel comfortable with each other. I show the sisters all of the groundwork exercises that I have done with the mare and how she responds to my signals as a rider. They do well together.

It is clear that they will need to continue working with the Mustang every day, but it is also clear that Mona will give back a lot to her owners in the future. I am happy with her owners; I think that they are a good match for the horse. I will also keep supporting them if they need my help.

When it's time for us to load Mona, it isn't easy for me as she leaves the farm. We both have a very intensive time of teaching and learning together behind us. Things will be different when she is no longer here. On the other hand, I am happy that she has found people who recognize that she is special and understand that there is still a long training journey ahead of them.

I wish this special horse and her people all the very best for the future!

POSTSCRIPT

I had never thought that I would change and grow so much as a result of an encounter with a horse. I am very grateful for the time that I spent with Mona. I definitely have more to learn from what we experienced together. During the time with the Mustang, my awareness intensified, especially for how horses think and how they see things. It also encouraged me to rethink common training methods. And I would like to encourage you to do the same!

Even if not everybody has the opportunity to work with a Mustang, I would like to advise all horsemen and women to keep broadening their horizons, questioning their actions, and thinking beyond existing boundaries and norms.

I would also encourage you to support projects that help animals—no matter what species. I put my time and energy into the cause of the Mustangs of North America, whose fate I will continue to champion in the future. I am very happy to have been able to help some wild horses onto a path toward a happy home, even if it was just a few. Makeover events have put a spotlight on these very special horses. I hope that they might inspire more people to get involved and help the Mustangs.

ACKNOWLEDGMENTS

I would like to thank everyone who is dedicated to the well-being of animals, both in their own country and abroad. In particular, I would like to thank the people behind "American Mustang Germany" for bringing this project to life.

I would like to thank my German publishers, Müller Rüschlikon, for trusting me to write about this special project.

I am also grateful to everybody who has supported me behind the scenes, especially my family, my parents, and my husband, who always back me up on my decisions and encourage me in whatever I do.

Special thanks also go to my good friend Joanna who was such a help to me. I never have a big team with me at events, because I only need a few important people I can completely rely on, and that includes you!

Last, but not least, I would like to thank the incredibly special horse I write about in these pages. I learned so much from you, Mona. I will use what I have learned to help others like you, and I will pass on my knowledge.

Thank you!

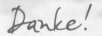

INDEX

Page numbers in *italics* indicate illustrations.